Teaching Reading Strategies
in the School Library

Teaching Reading Strategies in the School Library

Christine Walker
Sarah Shaw

Westport, Connecticut • London

Library of Congress Cataloging-in-Publication Data

Walker, Christine, 1966–
 Teaching reading strategies in the school library / Christine Walker and Sarah Shaw.
   p. cm.
 Includes bibliographical references and index.
 ISBN 1–59158–120–6 (pbk. : alk. paper)
 1. Elementary school libraries—Activity programs—United States. 2. Reading (Elementary)—Activity programs. I. Shaw, Sarah, 1975– II. Title.
Z675.S3W193 2004
027.8′222—dc22   2004048643

British Library Cataloguing in Publication Data is available.

Copyright © 2004 by Libraries Unlimited

All rights reserved. No portion of this book may be reproduced, by any process or technique, without the express written consent of the publisher.

Library of Congress Catalog Card Number: 2004048643
ISBN: 1–59158–120–6

First published in 2004

Libraries Unlimited, 88 Post Road West, Westport, CT 06881
A Member of the Greenwood Publishing Group, Inc.
www.lu.com

Printed in the United States of America

The paper used in this book complies with the Permanent Paper Standard issued by the National Information Standards Organization (Z39.48–1984).

10 9 8 7 6 5 4 3

For three great storytellers, Dad, Bill, and Dylan. C. W.

To Anne, who was along for the wild ride. S. S.

Contents

Acknowledgments ix

Chapter 1   Strategies   1

Building Interest   9

Chapter 2   Prediction Word Bank   11
Chapter 3   Character Chart   25
Chapter 4   KWL Chart   33

Retelling   39

Chapter 5   Sequence   41
Chapter 6   Circular Sequence Story Chart   55
Chapter 7   Goal Structure Map   63
Chapter 8   Story Element Map   77

Compare and Contrast   93

Chapter 9   T-Table   95
Chapter 10   Venn Diagram   107

Comprehension   117

Chapter 11   Q.A.R. (Question–Answer Relationship)   119

Appendix   135

References   143

Index   145

Acknowledgments

Thanks to Mary Ellen Grant for first seeing the potential of this idea *and* for encouraging us to share it with others.

In addition to envisioning a book hidden in a presentation, we are grateful to Sharon Coatney for her editorial guidance.

For her photography expertise (and patience) on a very blustery day we are thankful to Melanie DeMoss.

To our families, friends, and colleagues we want to express our appreciation for their never-ending support and encouragement.

And last but not least . . . thanks to the students at Arbor Creek, Regency Place, and Fairview for serving as willing guinea pigs. They are always a source of inspiration and motivation for our efforts.

CHAPTER

Strategies

THE RATIONALE

The concept of this book came from a desire to make a difference in the reading achievement of primary students (K–3rd grade) in an elementary school setting. With the increasing demands on classroom teachers, it is abundantly clear that all staff members must do their part to help increase reading success. Given the limited time that library media specialists have with students, how can that time be used best to increase reading achievement?

Much has been written about the benefits derived from the promotion of independent reading, author studies, and genre exploration for reading success. We agree these are all wonderful tools for improving student interaction with literature. It is our suggestion, however that library media specialists can use their time with students to model and reinforce research-based reading strategies commonly used in the classroom. Most of these activities can be conducted within a matter of just a few minutes during a library storytime while promoting independent reading, author studies, and genre exploration at the same time.

Given the nature of a library storytime, it was important to us that these activities be flexible and adaptable so they can quickly be changed as new groups of students are ushered in and out of the library media center. By creating reusable chart templates, these reading strategies can be conducted with a variety of stories. After the initial creation of the charts, only the supporting material will need to be created as they are used with different pieces of literature. Over one hundred newly published books are highlighted in this text that work well with each of the ten strategies explored.

HOW IS THIS BOOK ORGANIZED?

The Strategies

Each of the ten reading strategies are highlighted in separate chapters outlined next. The chapters appear in the text grouped into four sections according to their function: Building Interest, Retelling, Compare and Contrast, and Comprehension.

Building Interest

Example of layout without graphics	
<div align="center">**Prediction Word Chart**</div>	
Characters	Setting
Plot	I think this story will be about...

Figure 1.1 Prediction Word Bank. This strategy builds vocabulary, strengthens prediction skills, and helps review story elements. Before reading a text, students discuss and sort vocabulary from the book into three different categories; setting, characters, and plot. After all words are sorted, students begin to make predictions about what they think the story may be about, largely based on the vocabulary that has been introduced.

Example of layout without graphics	
<div align="center">**Character Chart**</div>	
List all the attributes or characteristics that you think a _____ might possess.	
Before Reading What attributes might they possess?	**After Reading** Which attributes were present in the story?

Figure 1.2 Character Chart. This strategy builds anticipation for the story while encouraging students to verbalize character attributes. Before reading the story, students are asked to list common traits of a particular character based on prior knowledge about certain types of individuals that they have met in stories before. Based on the attributes listed, students are asked to make a prediction about what might happen in the new piece of literature.

Figure 1.3 KWL. This graphic organizer is useful for activating prior knowledge as well as helping students anticipate what may be found in an expository text. Before reading the text, students record information they already "know" about a topic and what they "want to learn" about the subject. After the story is shared, students record what they have "learned" from the text.

Retelling

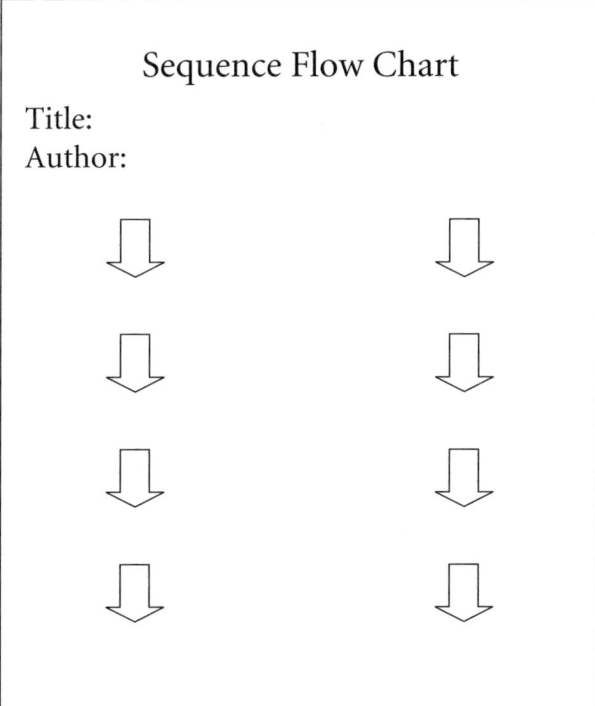

Figure 1.4 Sequence. This strategy helps students develop a sense of story as they retell the order of events from the text. Using pictures, words, or phrases children place items in the correct sequence after the story is completed, developing on their retelling skills.

4 Strategies

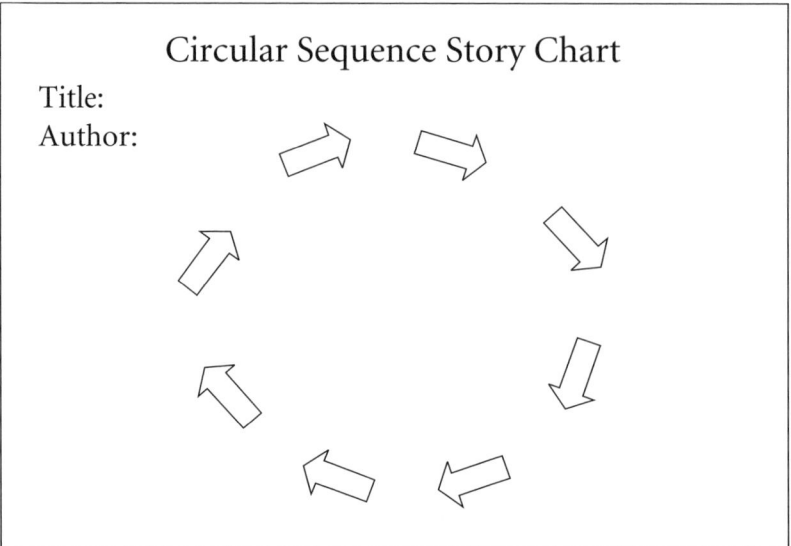

Figure 1.5 Circular Sequence. This strategy has the same benefits as sequence, which includes development of story sense as well as retelling skills. The unique aspect of the circular sequence strategy is that it is used with pieces of literature that have a plot that ends where the story first began. Using circular charts, students are able to visualize the more abstract elements of the plot.

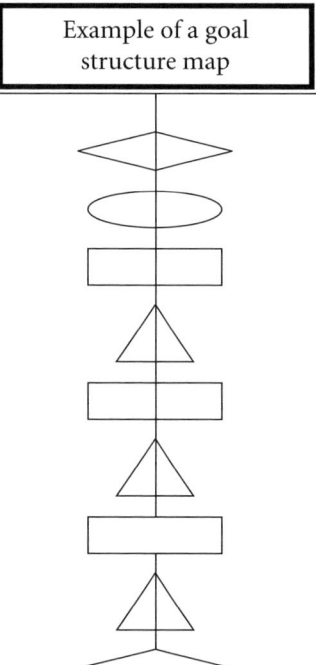

Figure 1.6 Goal Structure Map. This graphic representation helps readers understand the connections between the important story units by looking at the main character's ultimate goal and the attempts he/she made to reach the goal. It gives readers a chance to reflect on the feelings, thoughts, and actions of the character.

Example of layout without graphics

Story Element Map

Title: Author:

Characters	Setting
Problem	Solution

Figure 1.7 Story Element Map. This strategy encourages students to develop summarization skills and a sense of story as they focus on the important elements of the text, not the unimportant details. After the story has been read, students are asked to identify the setting, characters, problem, and solution.

Compare and Contrast

T-Table

Figure 1.8 T-Table. This graphic organizer is used to sort and categorize information from the story. By manipulating language, students are asked to make sense of information they have received from the text in a systematic way.

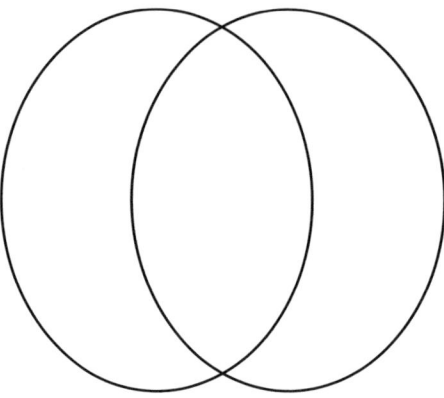

Venn Diagram

Figure 1.9 Venn Diagram. This graphic organizer provides readers with the opportunity to compare and contrast characteristics of stories visually by using two intersecting circles. By reflecting on the similarities and differences two stories have regarding plot lines, characters, settings, and thematic elements, students bring abstract ideas into the concrete realm.

Comprehension

Example of layout without graphics		
Right There		Think and Search
Title:	**Q.A.R.** Question–Answer Relationship	Author:
Author and You		On Your Own

Figure 1.10 Question–Answer Relationship. This strategy teaches students to analyze the task demands of different types of questions. By deciding what type of question is being asked, readers will know where to go to get the information needed to answer it. By utilizing this strategy students will be able to increase their success answering comprehension questions as they sort questions into four categories: *Right There, Think and Search, Author and You*, and *On Your Own*.

THE DESIGN

Within each chapter you will find four sections indicated by icons, but in the case of the *Integrate It!* section by book cover artwork.

KNOW IT!

This section explains the strategy and the benefits of its use with students.

CREATE IT!

This section explains how to create the chart, graphic organizer, and literature elements you will need to use the strategy with students. It may include items you will need to reproduce as you create.

INTEGRATE IT!

This section provides actual lessons to use with specific pieces of literature. Pages can be reproduced and used with students immediately.

LINK IT!

This section provides a brief summary of newly published literature that works well with the strategy because of the design of the plot. You will find 130 different books highlighted.

An appendix at the end of the book will provide you with a complete list of all of the literature that appears in the text.

Building Interest

CHAPTER

Prediction Word Bank

As readers, we constantly make and confirm or discount guesses about what we think will unfold in the text. We use context clues, world knowledge, and knowledge of language, along with ways of solving words visually to form hypotheses as we read.

Mosaic of Thought, Keene and Zimmerman, 1997

KNOW IT!

A Prediction Word Bank (Benson and Cummins, 2000) builds vocabulary, strengthens prediction skills, and reviews story elements. Before hearing the story, students get the opportunity to interact with vocabulary that will appear in the selection. They help to sort the vocabulary from the story into different categories; characters, setting, and plot. As the sorting process takes place, students and instructor are discussing any unfamiliar words before placing them on the chart. After all words are sorted, students begin to make predictions about what they think the story may be about, largely based on the vocabulary that has been introduced.

CREATE IT!

Using a large poster board, divide the sheet into the appropriate number of box areas as shown. Attach the text headings: PREDICTION WORD BANK; CHARACTERS; SETTING; PLOT; and I THINK THIS STORY WILL BE ABOUT . . . . Pre-read the book that will be shared, selecting vocabulary from the text that may be unfamiliar to students, yet will help them make a prediction about the story. Be sure to gather words for all three of the categories; characters, setting, and plot. The vocabulary that pertains to the characters and setting can be adjectives that would describe them, as well as nouns that name them. Plot vocabulary can be any words that pertain to the events and action in the story. After the words are gathered, type up the vocabulary and laminate the paper as well as the reusable poster board. Cut words apart for students to use.

Introduce the story to students by discussing the front-cover artwork. Explain that they are going to examine some of the vocabulary from inside the book to make predictions. Let them know they must decide if the vocabulary word may give information about the characters, setting, or plot. Ask volunteers to attach the word using tacky adhesive in the appropriate box, discussing any unfamiliar vocabulary as the need arises. After all words have been categorized and discussed, ask a few students to make some predictions as to what the story may be about. Use an overhead marker to record predictions in the I THINK THIS STORY WILL BE ABOUT . . . box. These predictions can be quickly erased with a wet tissue when it is time to move to a new story. After sharing the story with students, refer back to the Prediction Word Bank and quickly reflect on the predictions students offered before the story was read. Be sure to reassure students that predictions do not have to be absolutely correct, but rather educated guesses.

Example of layout without graphics	
Prediction Word Bank	
Characters	Setting
Plot	I think this story will be about…

Figure 2.1 Example of chart.

Prediction Word Bank

Setting

Characters

I think this story will be about…

Plot

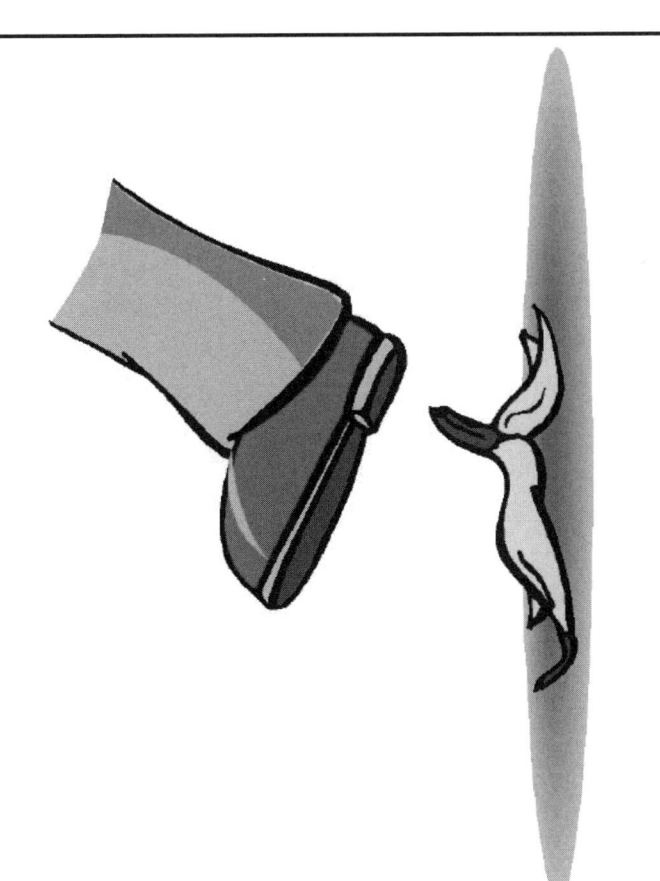

INTEGRATE IT!

Now take the following *two* titles and try it for yourself.

The Lizard Man of Crabtree County
Written by Lucy Nolan • Illustrated by Jill Kastner

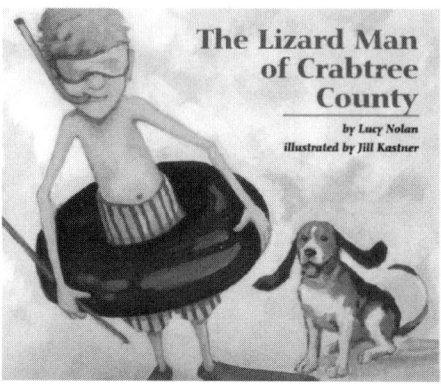

Figure 2.2 *The Lizard Man of Crabtree County.* Reprinted with permission of Marshall Cavendish Children's Books.

Nothing exciting ever happens in Crabtree County until the day Mrs. Bunch spots a mysterious lizard man. James Arthur hears the rumor about the strange creature on the same day he decides to dress up as a bush so something exciting will happen to him. The boy is amazed that he didn't run into the monster at the pond because apparently they were both there at the same time. He is never at the right place at the right time . . . or so he thinks!

The Lizard Man of Crabtree County
Written by Lucy Nolan

Lizard Man	Moondog
firemen	Crabtree County
summer	pond

shrub	plastered
tracking gear	gooey
howled	clever
spine-tingling wail	Sammy-the-Sea-Serpent float

Miss Alaineus—A Vocabulary Disaster
Written and illustrated by Debra Frasier

Figure 2.3 *Miss Alaineus—A Vocabulary Disaster* © 2000 by Debra Frasier. Used with permission of Harcourt Publishing.

Sage experiences the sting of embarrassment when she makes a mistake with a vocabulary word in front of her classmates. Fortunately, she is able to use her quick wit and ingenuity to turn an embarrassing situation around by bravely participating in the Vocabulary Parade. This is a touching story that celebrates the wonders of the English language.

 **LINK IT!**

Try linking some of these newly published titles to this reading strategy.

Lucky Socks
Written by Carrie Weston • Illustrated by Charlotte Middleton

Kevin's day always seems to be full of trouble when he wears any color of socks but his yellow pair. On the days when he wears his lucky yellow socks, things always seem to go Kevin's way. Field day at school arrives and Kevin can't find his yellow socks. He looks everywhere but can't locate them. Mom suggests that he wear something else yellow to the special event at school. Will Kevin's day be trouble free without his good luck charms?

The Perfect Pet
Written by Carol Chataway • Illustrated by Greg Holfeld

Hamlet, Pygmalion, and Podge are three pigs with a problem. They want a dog but they are unsure of what kind of dog they desire. Mr. Pinkerton tries to solve their problem by letting them take dogs from the pet store to test out. Unfortunately, all of the "test" dogs never seem to work out quite right. They go revisit Mr. Pinkerton certain they will never find a suitable pet, but luckily he comes up with a solution that makes them all happy.

Miss Alaineus
A Vocabulary Disaster

Written and illustrated by
Debra Frasier

Miss Alaineus	Miss Stake
Webster School	Vocabulary Day
Sage	scribble

definitions	costumes
grinned	embarrassment
miscellaneous	devastated
ancestor	astonishment
parade	humbled

Max
Written and illustrated by Bob Graham

Max comes from a family of high-flying superheroes. But even with special instruction from his parents, Captain Lightning and Madam Thunderbolt, Max can't seem to lift off from the ground. It is only after he is forced to come to the aid of a falling baby bird that he is inspired to learn to fly.

Water Hole Waiting
Written by Jane and Christopher Kurtz • Illustrated by Lee Christiansen

A thirsty monkey waits as the larger animals in the jungle drink from the water hole on the African savanna. Because they are the most vulnerable of the animals that use the hole, the monkey and his family have to wait while the hippos, zebras, elephants, and various other creatures get their sips. When the sun finally sinks in the sky, the monkey's family gets their long awaited turn.

Clara Caterpillar
Written by Pamela Duncan Edwards • Illustrated by Henry Cole

Clara the caterpillar is a common cabbage caterpillar. On the other hand, Catisha is a beautiful crimson caterpillar who uses her catty disposition to remind Clara she will never be a colorful butterfly like Catisha. Clara shows her other winning qualities though when she helps distract a crow from eating Catisha for dinner. Clara's courage and camouflage techniques are a powerful combination. Alliterative language makes this selection perfect for vocabulary development and exploration.

Old Cricket
Written by Lisa Wheeler • Illustrated by Ponder Goembel

Old Cricket woke up with a creak in his knee, a crick in his neck, and a crack in his back. His "ailments" prevent him from helping his relatives with the chores. As he makes his way to Doc Hopper's residence his clever plan for a restful afternoon is soon interrupted by the caw-caw-caw of the hungry Crow. This story is full of rich vocabulary and wordplay associated with the letter "c."

Rosie's Roses
Written by Pamela Duncan Edwards • Illustrated by Henry Cole

Using alliterative language related to the letter "r," this story follows Rosie on a romp through the forest. She is on a mission to give her Aunt Ruth a birthday present of four roses tied with a rainbow ribbon. Unfortunately, a rose robber must be on the loose because the roses begin to disappear, rose by rose. Will Rosie realize the intrinsic reward of sharing?

The Wolf Who Cried Boy
Written by Bob Hartman • Illustrated by Tim Raglin

Little Wolf is tired of eating the same old meals for dinner. He is tired of munching on lamburgers and sloppy does when what he really wants to eat is boy. True to the spirit of *The Boy Who Cried Wolf* this hilarious twisted tale has Little Wolf tricking his parents into thinking he has seen a boy in the woods and starting a wild hunt. What will happen when a real boy comes along?

The Web Files
Written by Margie Palatini • Illustrated by Richard Egielski

Ducktective Web and his partner are investigating a case of pilfered almost-pickled peppers. Can they quack the case of the pepper pincher? The suspects include a multitude of familiar nursery rhyme characters including Little Boy Blue, Jack Horner, and the Three Blind Mice. Fun word play makes this hilarious tale a real delight.

Dear Mrs. LaRue: Letters from Obedience School
Written and illustrated by Mark Teague

Ike, a dog with a talent for writing letters, has been sent to obedience school by his owner Gertrude LaRue. It seems Ike has been stealing food off of plates, chasing the neighbor's cats, and disturbing folks with his howling. From obedience school Ike begins sending his owner letters trying to convince her that he has been unjustly accused and poorly treated in "prison." After a daring escape from detention, Ike redeems himself with a heroic deed.

Arnie the Doughnut
Cooked up by Laurie Keller

Arnie the talking doughnut is shocked to find out that he has been created to be eaten. He tries to convince his owner Mr. Bing that he might be good for something other than a snack, perhaps as a personal trainer, chauffeur, or a bodyguard. Mr. Bing suggests that maybe Arnie could be his pincushion, air freshener, or a paperweight. Just when it seems they will need to part ways because they don't seem to be able to compromise on a job, a suitable solution is suggested. Arnie can become the first doughnut-dog!

CHAPTER

Character Chart

Character mapping helps children identify main characters and think about how their attributes influence the development of a story.

Supporting Struggling Readers, Walker, 1992

KNOW IT!

Completing a Character Chart (Benson and Cummins, 2000) not only allows students to discuss attributes of individuals in literature, but it also can be a terrific way to practice prediction skills. This graphic organizer asks readers to list common characteristics of a particular character, for example a king, janitor, rat, or bully. Based on the attributes listed, students are asked to make a prediction about what might happen in the piece of literature. After the story is read, students confirm whether the attribute they predicted would be in the text met their expectations. This is not only a great strategy for building anticipation for the story, but also for encouraging students to verbalize the characteristics typically associated with certain characters. They have to activate their prior knowledge about certain types of individuals that they have met in stories before so they can make assumptions about the new characters they are about to meet.

CREATE IT!

Using a magic marker draw a two column, multi-row chart on poster board as shown. Attach text headings in the appropriate boxes—CHARACTER CHART; BEFORE READING; and AFTER READING. It will be necessary to laminate the poster board because an overhead pen will be used to record information.

Select a story that has a character that students can be successful generating attributes for. This graphic organizer works particularly well with stories where the attributes of the character play an important role in the plot of the story. Before completing the character chart it is necessary to have a discussion regarding what character attributes are, including the type of descriptive language required. It might be helpful to do some brainstorming on a common character, like a princess for example, before actually completing a Character Chart activity for a piece of literature.

Once students have been introduced to character attributes, show them the front-cover artwork for the story to be shared. Indicate what type of character is involved in the plot. Ask students to generate a list of characteristics they think this individual might possess based on the cover and their prior knowledge from other pieces of literature.

Example of layout without graphics

Character Chart

List all the attributes or characteristics that you think a _____ might possess.

Before Reading What attributes might they possess?	**After Reading** Which attributes were present in the story?

Figure 3.3 Example of chart.

In the BEFORE READING column, record this information on the chart with an overhead pen that can be erased with a wet paper towel after the session. Set a reason for reading by telling students they need to be listening carefully as the story is read because they will need to be able to confirm whether their prediction was present in the text or not. After the story is shared, read down the list of attributes and ask students to indicate whether a "+" or "−" should be placed in the AFTER READING column. A "+" indicates that the character did indeed possess the characteristic in the text. A "−" indicates that the individual did not display the listed attribute.

Character Chart

27

Before Reading	**After Reading**	
What attributes might they possess?	Which attributes were present in the story?	List all the attributes or characteristics that you think a _____ might possess.

INTEGRATE IT!

Now take the following *two* titles and try it for yourself.

The Bugliest Bug
Written by Carol Diggory Shields • Illustrated by Scott Nash

Figure 3.2 *The Bugliest Bug*. Text © 2002 by Carol Diggory Shields. Illustrations © 2002 by Scott Nash. Reproduced by permission of the publisher Candlewick Press, Inc., Cambridge, MA.

All of the insects are excited about the contest that will name one of them the "Bugliest Bug" of them all. The crickets, click beetles, and ladybugs all take the stage to demonstrate their special skills. But Dilly the Damselfly begins to question the true motivations of the contest judges. Perhaps they are up to no good!

Porcupining: A Prickly Love Story
Written by Lisa Wheeler • Illustrated by Jane Bynum

Cushion is a lonely porcupine who is desperate for someone to love. It seems no one is very interested in him at the petting zoo because no one wants to pet a porcupine. Cushion decides it is time to do something about it so he takes his banjo and begins to serenade other animals in the zoo to find someone to be his true love. After many failed attempts he finally finds Barbara, a prickly hedgehog who is also looking for some passion in her lonely love life.

LINK IT!

Try linking some of these newly published titles to this reading strategy.

That Pesky Rat
Written and illustrated by Lauren Child

That pesky rat is tired of his dirty alley and lonely lifestyle so he is looking for a comfortable home. He feels he is ready to become someone's pet so he can finally have a proper name, rather than "that pesky rat." He visits the pet store to ask if they think anyone would want to adopt him. Luckily for this pesky rat someone comes along with poor eyesight and decides to take the "kitty" home.

Snowmen at Night
Written by Caralyn Buehner • Illustrated by Mark Buehner

Have you ever wondered what snowmen do at night? These snowpeople gather together and have snowball fights, giant baseball games, and ice-skating races. They spend the evening drinking hot cocoa after a night full of sledding. Maybe that's why they don't look quite the same in the morning as they did when you left them the night before.

Can You Do This Old Badger?
Written by Eve Bunting • Illustrated by Le Uyen Pham

Even though Old Grandpa Badger is not as quick and limber as he use to be, he can still teach Little Badger a few things. Old Badger spends an afternoon in the forest explaining the finer points of napping, fishing, and eating.

The Feet in the Gym
Written by Terri Daniels • Illustrated by Travis Foster

Handy Bob the janitor at Lakeside School is responsible for many things but the most important job he has is keeping the gym floor clean. It is not an easy task with all the kids that trample in and out. Rhyming text helps to illustrate the hard work and patience a custodian must possess.

Crackers
Written by Becky Bloom • Illustrated by Pascal Biet

Crackers is a cat that can't seem to hold down a job. Every job he is hired for he finds himself eventually fired from. He is constantly being terminated because he won't be mean to mice. Crackers is devastated until being kind to the mice finally pays off. There is a job opening at the locally mouse-owned cheese shop. All of the mice who Crackers has helped persuade the owner to give the cat a chance at employment.

The Recess Queen
Written by Alexis O'Neill • Illustrated by Laura Huliska-Beith

This is the story of mean Jean the recess queen. Everybody follows mean Jean's lead before they will do anything on the playground. One day a new kid comes to school, Katie Sue, who won't wait for mean Jean to call the shots. When Katie Sue stands up to Jean a lesson in friendship is learned.

The Ant Bully
Written and illustrated by John Nickle

Sid the Bully is always picking on Lucas because of his unique glasses and funny hat. Consequently Lucas takes his aggression out on a colony of innocent ants. One day the six-legged creatures capture Lucas and shrink him, sentencing their prisoner to manual labor.

City Chicken
Written Arthur Dorros • Illustrated by Henry Cole

Henrietta is a chicken who has always lived in the city. Having never visited the country, she decides to take a trip to find out what horses, pigs, cows, and (of course) chickens do on the grounds of a quiet country farm. Imagine Henrietta's surprise to find her poultry friends confined to tiny individual cages as motors and gears move their newly laid eggs down conveyor belts to paper cartons.

New York's Bravest
Written by Mary Pope Osborne • Illustrated by Steve Johnson and Lou Fancher

In this urban tall tale about a firefighter named Mose Humphreys, the main character performs many heroic deeds for the people of New York. After one dangerous blaze Mose is nowhere to be found. Much speculation is made about the hero's whereabouts, but soon it is decided they know where he is. Mose resides in all firefighter's hearts and minds as they battle blaze after blaze.

Big Bad Wolf
Written by Claire Masurel • Illustrated by Melissa Iwai

The Big Bad Wolf has a reputation for having a piercing howl that will frighten any child. But in reality he is a family man who would rather go on picnics and smother his children with goodnight kisses.

CHAPTER four

KWL Chart

Learning to use their own background knowledge to help decode text is often difficult for struggling readers who don't realize how much they already know and view each new reading situation as starting from scratch to learn completely unknown information.

Supporting Struggling Readers, Walker, 1992

KNOW IT!

KWL charts (Ogle, 1989) are useful tools for activating prior knowledge when exploring expository text. Readers will be more successful at making sense of new information, if they have begun to think about what they already know about a subject. In addition, KWL charts build a sense of excitement prior to text being read because students will get to share what they already know about a particular subject. It gets them anticipating what information may be found in the text.

A KWL chart not only asks the reader to look at what they already know about a subject, it also asks them to look at what questions they would like answered from a text. By examining what they "know" and envisioning what they "want" to gain from the text, students are primed with a purpose to read. After the text is read, information is recorded that indicates what facts were gathered from the book. Be aware that often there are questions that students have generated that are not answered in the text at all. Students can be encouraged to research the answers in other texts or simply be told that not all books will answer all questions. Many sources may need to be consulted to get the information desired.

CREATE IT!

Although a KWL chart can be created individually by students, the confines of library time usually dictate that it be developed as a whole group. Using simply drawn visual images to organize the three sections of the KWL chart will maintain student interest and make for a great prize to give away to a lucky listener after the chart is complete. After deciding on the image(s), draw it on a large piece of butcher or chart paper with magic marker. Label three distinct areas with "KNOW," "WANT TO LEARN," and "LEARNED."

After selecting an expository text to share with students, introduce them to the topic of the book and ask them to share what they already know about the subject. Record this information on the chart. It is important that this information is recorded without judgment because all readers will come to the text with varying levels of expertise. Next, ask students to generate some questions they have about the subject. It is a good idea to have them think about what questions may be answered in the text based on the cover, headings, illustrations, and table of contents. This may serve to focus their questions, but again, all inquiries are accepted without judgment. Record these questions on the chart in the appropriate section.

Before reading the text aloud, reread what information students have contributed to the KWL chart. This serves to activate prior knowledge and sets up a purpose for reading the text. After the book is read, record information that students have gathered in the appropriate space on the chart. These facts may or may not answer the questions students posed before reading the text. Accept all correct information and reassure students that not all books will answer all the questions they may have on a topic: sometimes a reader may have to go to other resources to find specific information.

It is important to note that with primary-school age children, the recording of knowledge, questions, and facts can go on for a very long period of time. It is advisable to set a limit on the number of answers you will be recording for each section so the chart can be completed in one class setting and student interest remains high.

INTEGRATE IT!

Now take the following *four* titles and try it for yourself.

Dinosaur Bones
Written and illustrated by Bob Barner

Figure 4.1   Example of KWL Chart based on original art by Bob Barner.

Figure 4.2   From *Dinosaur Bones* © 2001 by Bob Barner. Used with permission of Chronicle Books LLC, San Francisco. *ChronicleBooks.com*

Paper-collage illustrations make dinosaur facts come to life for dino lovers everywhere. Rhyming text leads readers through the fossil remains of dinosaur bones and shows how they lived their life on earth. More in-depth information is provided on each page for dinosaur enthusiasts who crave more facts on these fascinating creatures.

Apples
Written and illustrated by Gail Gibbons

Figure 4.3 Apples copyright © 2000 by Gail Gibbons. Reprinted by permission of Holiday House, Inc.

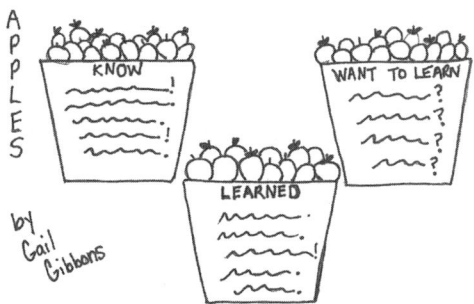

Figure 4.4 Example of KWL Chart based on original art by Gail Gibbons.

Readers learn about how an apple is formed, the different ways to use them, and how to identify different varieties. Detailed directions for making an apple pie and apple cider make this resource complete.

Supermarket
Written by Kathleen Krull • Illustrated by Melanie Hope Greenberg

Figure 4.5 Supermarket copyright © 2001 by Kathleen Krull, illustrated by Melanie Hope Greenberg. Reprinted by permission of Holiday House.

Figure 4.6 Example of KWL Chart based on original art by Kathleen Krull.

Did you know that bananas are the most popular fruit to be purchased in a supermarket? This book describes in great detail everything one could need to know about a supermarket. Readers can learn about all the different store sub-areas, the duties of supermarket employees, and interesting sales statistics. Information on the history of food preparation and distribution is included.

Chickens May Not Cross the Road and Other Crazy (But True) Laws
Written by Kathi Linz • Illustrated by Tony Griego

Figure 4.7 *Chickens May Not Cross the Road and Other Crazy But True Laws* by Kathi Linz, illustrated by Tony Griego. Jacket art copyright © 2002 by Tony Griego. Reprinted by permission of Houghton Mifflin Company. All rights reserved.

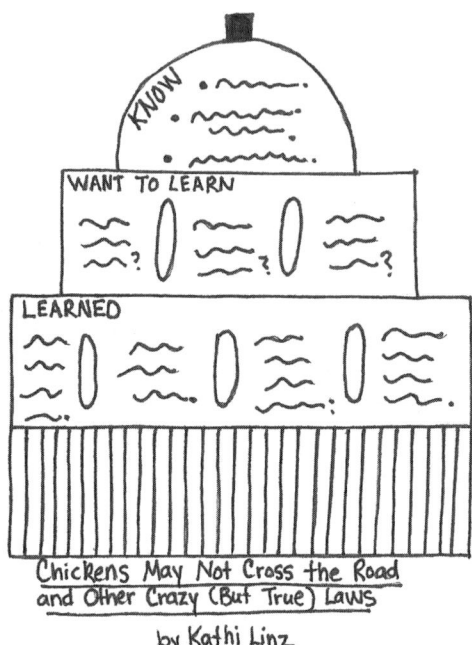

Figure 4.8 Example of KWL Chart based on original artwork by Kathi Linz.

"Monkeys Shall Not Ride on Buses" is a law in San Antonio, Texas. This fascinating collection of humorous laws from across the country will not only delight readers but also teach them about why laws exist and how they are established. Readers can also follow the sequence of steps that a bill must take to become a law.

 **LINK IT!**

Try linking some of these newly published titles to this reading strategy.

My Car
Written and Illustrated by Byron Barton

Sam takes care of his car and follows the traffic signs when driving. He can identify all the different parts of his car. The author uses very simple text to explain information about cars and driving to younger readers who are eager to begin reading non-fiction text.

My Fire Engine
Written and illustrated by Michael Rex

A little boy is playing with his toy fire engine imagining what it would be like to be a real firefighter. His imagination takes the reader through the exciting day of these tireless individuals. Experience the thrill of the fire alarm; the bravery of the men as they fight the fire with their equipment; and the relief of putting the fire engine away until the next emergency.

Red-Eyed Tree Frog
Written by Joy Cowley • Photos by Nic Bishop

Incredible close-up photography captures the day-to-day adventures of a tree frog. Follow this amphibian as he naps, searches for food, and avoids being a snake's dinner. Red-eyed tree frog facts in the back provide more in-depth information.

Waiting for Wings
Written and illustrated by Lois Ehlert

A group of patient caterpillars have been waiting for their butterfly wings. Follow their metamorphosis from egg to larva to chrysalis to butterfly. The author uses eye-popping illustrations, simple text, and unique page characteristics to share details of this insect's life. Deeper knowledge about butterfly anatomy, gardens, and identification can be obtained in the last section of the text.

My Soccer Book
Written and illustrated by Gail Gibbons

This book describes the basics of playing soccer. Using simple text the author describes the terminology, equipment, and the rules for how the game is played. Labeled diagrams explain soccer field areas and positions.

A Taste of Honey
Written and illustrated by Nancy Elizabeth Wallace

Through the curiosity of a young bear named Lily readers learn the step-by-step process of making honey. In addition to explaining the role bees play in the pollination process, the author describes all the equipment used to extract honey.

All You Need for a Snowman
Written by Alice Schertle • Illustrated by Barbara Lavallee

What do you need for a snowman? Rhyming text takes readers through the steps of creating a snowman. Follow a group of children as they wait for the first snowflake, create the perfect-size snowballs, and add decorations to their snowperson.

Bright Beetle
Written and illustrated by Rick Chrustowski

Follow the life cycle of a ladybug from an egg to fully developed adult. Readers learn what ladybugs eat, how they defend themselves, and what they do through the winter months.

The Emperor's Egg
Written by Martin Jenkins • Illustrated by Jane Chapman

Did you know when emperor penguins come into the world they survive thanks to the efforts of their father? Soon after laying an egg the mother penguin leaves and the father is responsible for keeping the egg warm. He does this by placing the egg on top of his feet and tucking it under his tummy. After patiently nurturing the egg for two long months, the egg hatches. Now he must take care of the chick and feed it until the mother returns. Interesting penguin facts are scattered through out text.

Retelling

CHAPTER

Sequence

Each child must listen to what has been told so far so that the retelling proceeds in a logical sequence. Sequencing helps readers rethink information in a logical order.

Comprehension: Strategic Instruction for K-3 Students, Owocki, 2003

KNOW IT!

Understanding the sequence of a story is crucial to comprehending the plot. When teaching sequence to primary students it is highly recommended to have a piece of literature that is repetitive in nature. As their level of reading comprehension increases, we can begin the process of moving our young readers from a concrete series of events to a more abstract series. In addition, exploring sequence not only improves story sense, but is also a superb device to use to practice retelling. When explaining the sequence of a story, the reader must retell all of the important events in his/her own words.

CREATE IT!

Primary-school age children can sequence or order events in a variety of ways, depending on the structure of the story. Often times the story can be introduced, shared, and sequenced in just one sitting. Or the instructor may choose to introduce and read the book in one session and use the sequence activity as a follow-up. In the latter case, the sequence activity can be used as a retelling device to very quickly assess comprehension of the important story elements before moving on to a related piece of literature.

In either sequencing scenario the anticipatory work is basically the same. Before reading the story aloud, explain to students that events in books happen in a certain order otherwise the story doesn't make sense. Ask them to listen to the sequence, or order, in the story very carefully because you will need some help after the story to put the events in the correct order.

If the book lends itself to using visuals, objects can be used to represent events of the story on a flannel board or pocket chart. Clip art can be used to represent items, characters, or events from the story. After the story has been shared, show students the visual images in a mixed-up fashion. Have students retell the story in order, placing the images in sequence as the retelling occurs.

Another way to illustrate sequence is to use a flow-chart template to help students see the order of events with the help of arrows. Events of the story are typed up, laminated, and cut up into large slips that can be viewed by the children while sitting in a rug area situation. Using a large piece of poster board, glue the heading information up at the top: SEQUENCE FLOW CHART, TITLE, and AUTHOR. Attach a series of arrows down the middle of the chart, leaving space between the arrows to place events of the story later. Laminate this chart template so it can be reused over and over again for other pieces of literature. After a book is shared, ask students to help retell the story in sequence by adding events to the chart as the group progresses through the story. These can be attached to the laminated chart with reusable tacky adhesive.

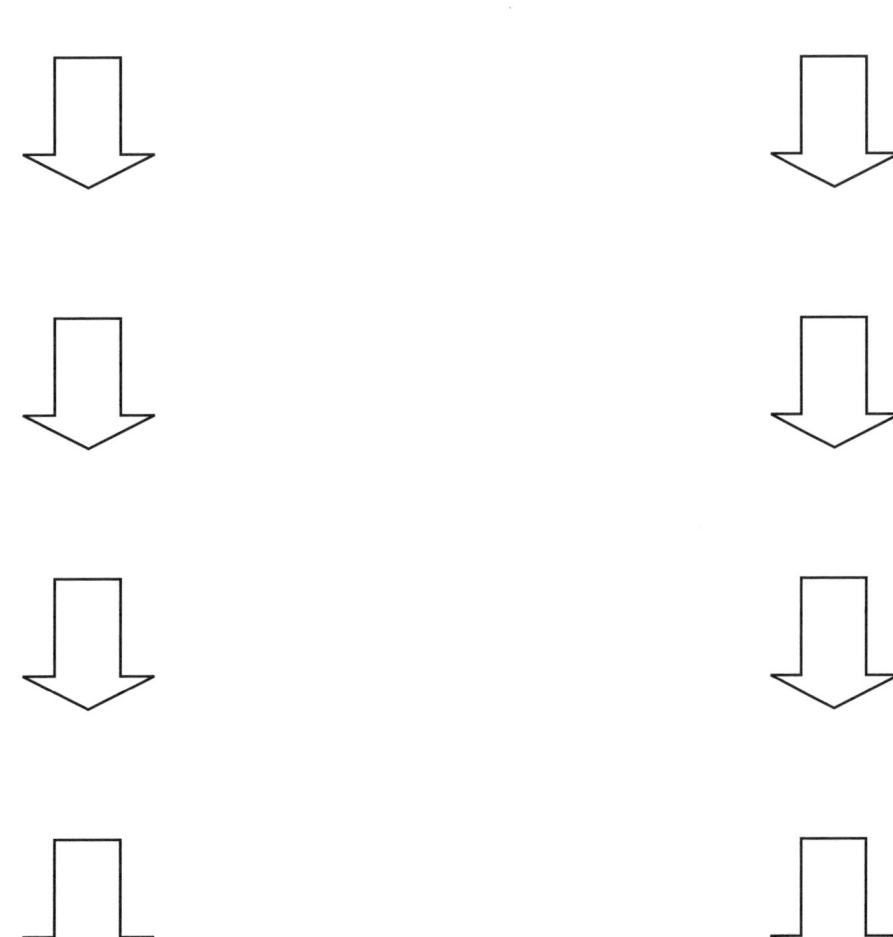

Figure 5.1 Example of chart.

Sequence Flow Chart

Title:

Author:

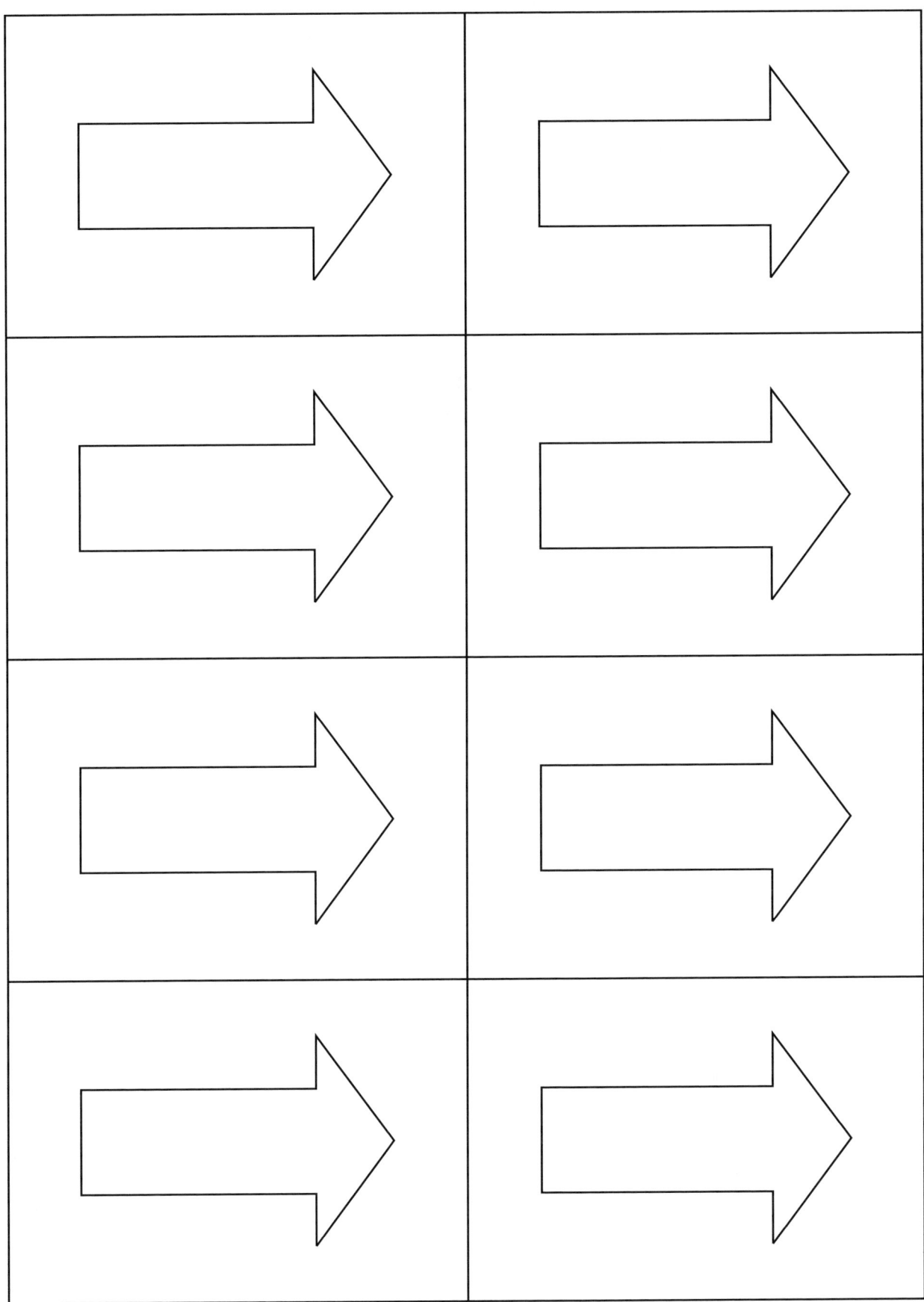

INTEGRATE IT!

Now take the following *two* titles and try it for yourself.

Henry Builds a Cabin
Written and illustrated by D.B. Johnson

Figure 5.2 *Henry Builds A Cabin* by D.B. Johnson. Jacket art copyright © 2002 by D.B. Johnson. Reprinted by permission of Houghton Mifflin Company. All rights reserved.

Young Henry begins cutting down trees so he can build a cabin. As the months go by friends stop to see the progress on Henry's cabin. Everyone comments on the size of the cabin. They believe it is too small to eat, read, or dance inside. But Henry is satisfied with the size of his abode because he cherishes nature and believes in using only what you absolutely need, including space. The story is based upon the philosophy of Henry David Thoreau, who constructed a cabin on the shores of Walden Pond.

Henry Builds a Cabin
Written and Illustrated by D.B. Johnson
Henry borrows an ax and cuts down twelve trees.
Henry cuts, notches, and raises the beams.
Henry uses the boards from an old shed for the floor, roof, and walls.
He puts a door and two windows on his cabin.
Henry uses a hammer to nail on shingles.
He moves into his cabin.
Henry eats beans in the dining room (bean patch), reads in the library (sunny spot), and dances down the grand stairway (the path to the pond).
He wears his "room" when it's raining.

Figure 5.3 Example of completed chart.

The Scarecrow's Hat
Written and illustrated by Ken Brown

Figure 5.4 Reprinted by permission of Ken Brown, author and illustrator. Published by Peachtree Publishers.

Chicken thinks Scarecrow's hat would make a nice nest. Scarecrow will only swap his hat for a walking stick. Chicken doesn't own a walking stick, but she knows someone who does. Maybe they would be willing to barter! So Chicken sets off to trade various items with Badger, Crow, Sheep, Owl, and Donkey so she can eventually obtain the hat.

The Scarecrow's Hat

Donkey wants feathers to flick flies away. He is willing to swap a blanket.

Owl wants to block the sun that keeps him awake. He is willing to swap glasses.

The Scarecrow's Hat

Crow wants wool to line her nest. She is willing to swap a ribbon.

Sheep wants glasses to watch for the wolf. She is willing to swap wool.

The Scarecrow's Hat

Scarecrow wants a walking stick to lean on. He is willing to swap his hat.

Badger wants a ribbon to tie his door open. He is willing to swap a walking stick.

The Scarecrow's Hat

Chicken wants the Scarecrow's hat for her nest. She is willing to swap her feathers.

Chicken is not willing to swap her new nest to Duck or anyone else!

LINK IT!

Try linking some of these newly published titles to this reading strategy.

Joseph Had a Little Overcoat
Written and illustrated by Simms Taback

Joseph had a little overcoat, but it was so full of holes that he made it into a jacket. Unfortunately, the jacket becomes old and worn out as well that he makes it into a vest. This cycle continues until all Joseph is left with is a button. Eventually he loses the button. With nothing left Joseph thinks of a way to remember the overcoat he had once loved. He writes a book about it.

Off We Go
Written by Jane Yolen • Illustrated by Laurel Molk

A series of woodland creatures leave the forest to visit Grandma. Using expressive sound words, the animals sing their way across the meadow. "Tipppity toe, hippity hop, diggity deep, slither slee, scritchity scratch, creepity crawl to wherever Grandma's house is found."

Bark, George
Written and illustrated by Jules Feiffer

George is a dog that has serious problems. Every time his Mom asks him to bark a different animal noise comes out. He meows, quacks, oinks, and moos instead of barking like a dog should. His mother takes him to the vet who discovers the problem. The doctor reaches deep down inside of George and begins pulling out all of the animals that George has swallowed.

This is the House That Jack Built
Written and illustrated by Simms Taback

This cumulative tale all begins with a stash of cheese in Jack's house. The cheese attracts a crew of rowdy occupants including a rat, cat, cow, dog, maid, farmer, and judge. Will Jack's house ever be the same after the commotion?

All in One Hour
Written by Susan Stevens Crummel • Concept and pictures by Dorothy Donohue

In this cumulative rhyming tale, a cat stalking a mouse starts a chase that involves a dogcatcher, a policeman, and even a bank robber. The wild chase takes place in the time span of one hour as illustrated with a time indicator on each page.

One Rainy Day
Written and illustrated by Valeri Gorbachev

When Pig arrives at Goat's house she is all wet. Goat asks why she didn't stop under a tree to wait for the rain to pass. Pig explains that she had stopped but had suddenly been joined by many other animals in ever increasing numbers. Goat begins to understand that the reason Pig is soaked is because there just wasn't enough room left under the tree. But the real reason behind Pig's damp state are all the puddles she jumped into after leaving the tree!

Bear Snores On
Written by Karma Wilson • Illustrated by Jane Chapman

As Bear sleeps through the storm a Mouse comes into his home to escape the cold, but Bear snores on. Soon Rabbit, Badger, Gopher, and Mole join him, but Bear snores on. The gathering continues to grow into a huge party. When Bear finally wakes up he is sad to have missed the fun. So the party begins again with Bear in attendance, but all the participants are sleepy, except the well-rested Bear.

One-Dog Canoe
Written by Mary Casanova • Illustrated by Ard Hoyt

A girl and her dog set out one morning for a trip in her little red canoe. What begins as a trip just for two turns into an adventure full of new friends. Beaver, Loon, Wolf, Bear, and Moose all decide they want to join in the fun and jump in the one-dog canoe. When Frog joins the group, the boat overturns and they all go for a swim!

Seals on the Bus
Written by Lenny Hort • Illustrated by G. Brian Karas

Young readers will love the animal-themed twist on the familiar song "The Wheels on the Bus." In this version not only are the seals boarding the bus, but also a sequence of zoo animals including tigers, geese, monkeys, snakes, and skunks. As each group of animals joins the fun on the bus, readers are encouraged to use corresponding sound words—errping, roaring, and honking along the way.

The Magic Hat
Written by Mem Fox • Illustrated by Tricia Tusa

A magic hat blows into town and lands on the heads of a sequence of villagers. Each touch of the magic hat turns the townspeople into a variety of animals: a toad, baboon, bear, kangaroo, and a giraffe. A wizard appears returning all the people to their normal state and placing the hat on his own head with surprising results. Beautiful rhyming text brings this charming tale to life.

The House in the Meadow
Written by Shutta Crum • Illustrated by Paige Billin-Frye

Using a unique twist on the familiar counting poem, this book follows the hard work of ten friends as they help build a house for a newly married couple. Along the way, five roofers, four plumbers, three electricians, two painters, and one inspector contribute their services to complete a house in time for a new baby to arrive.

Chapter Six

Circular Sequence Story Chart

Sequencing activities help children make discoveries about how authors organize texts. Knowing about organization is key to locating ideas in text and to discovering what the author thinks is important.

Comprehension: Strategic Instruction for K-3 Students, Owocki, 2003

KNOW IT!

Every once in awhile a story is discovered that is written in such a way that the end becomes the beginning! A Circular Sequence Story Chart helps students to visually discover the circular nature of the text by presenting the events in a circle or pie shape. Readers are asked to place the events of the story in order while practicing their retelling skills. After the chart is complete students can use this graphic organizer to bring the abstract elements of plot design to a more concrete level.

CREATE IT!

A Circular Sequence Story Chart can be designed in two ways: Velcro pie or arrow circle. In either case it is suggested that the story being used is retold in eight steps so the templates can be reused. This may require combining an event or two. If it is a shorter story, a secondary event may need to be included. Additional templates with more or less spaces could be created if desired.

To create a Velcro pie chart, draw a large circle on a piece of poster board. Attach the text for the chart: CIRCULAR SEQUENCE STORY CHART; AUTHOR; TITLE. Using another piece of tagboard or poster board, draw another circle the same size. Cut the second circle out. Using a yardstick, divide the second circle into eight equal pieces. These are the eight event cards. Cut them into slices. For each different story retelling additional circles will need to be created. Attach Velcro behind each pie slice and a corresponding Velcro piece on the original circle poster board template. Clip art, words, and/or phrases can be attached to the Velcro slices.

To create an arrow circle chart, attach the text for the chart to the top of a piece of poster board: CIRCULAR SEQUENCE STORY CHART; AUTHOR; TITLE. Arrange and attach the arrows in a circular pattern around the board. On small rectangle cards place clip art, words, and/or phrases from the story. Laminate all items for reuse.

The procedure for using either chart is the same. Indicate to students that they need to be careful listeners as the story is shared because they will be required to put

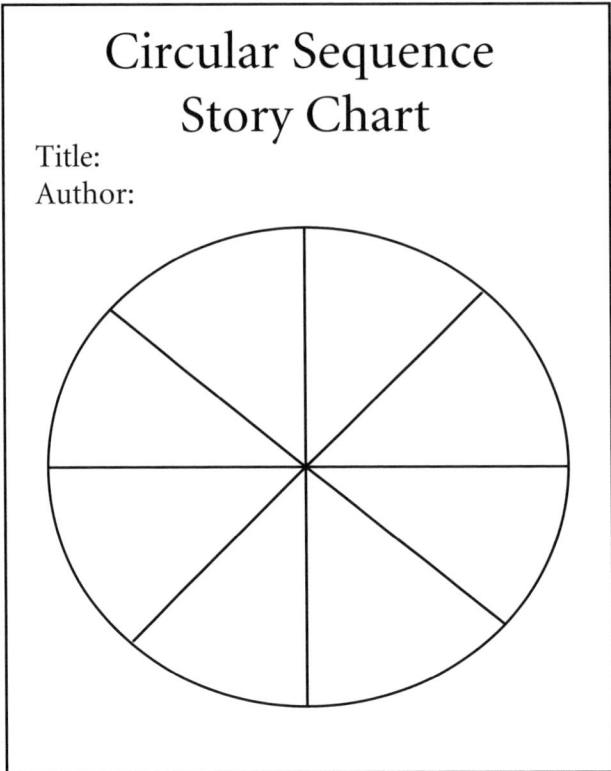

Figure 6.1 Example of Velcro pie story map.

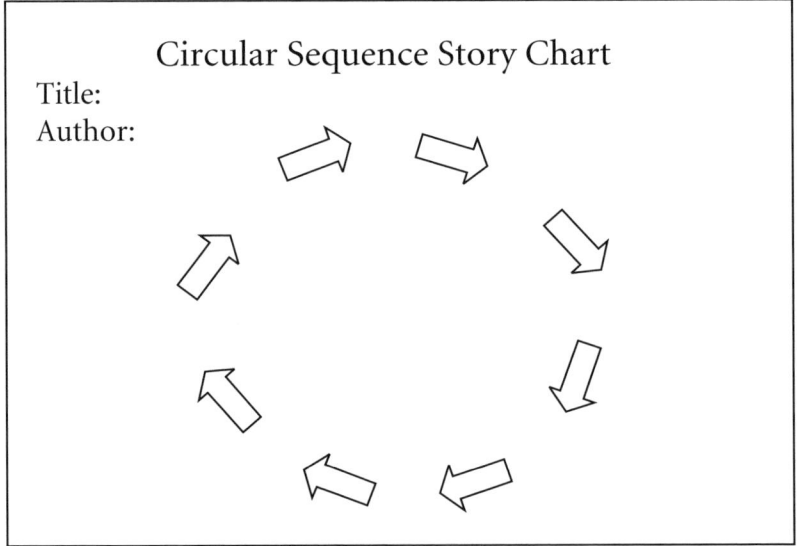

Figure 6.2 Example of an arrow circle map.

the story in sequence. After reading the story and discussing the circular nature of the plot, ask students to retell the story. Helpers can place the events around the circle charts as the story is retold. When the circle or pie is complete, students will be able to visually connect how the story could start around the circle again.

Circular Sequence Story Chart

Title:

Author:

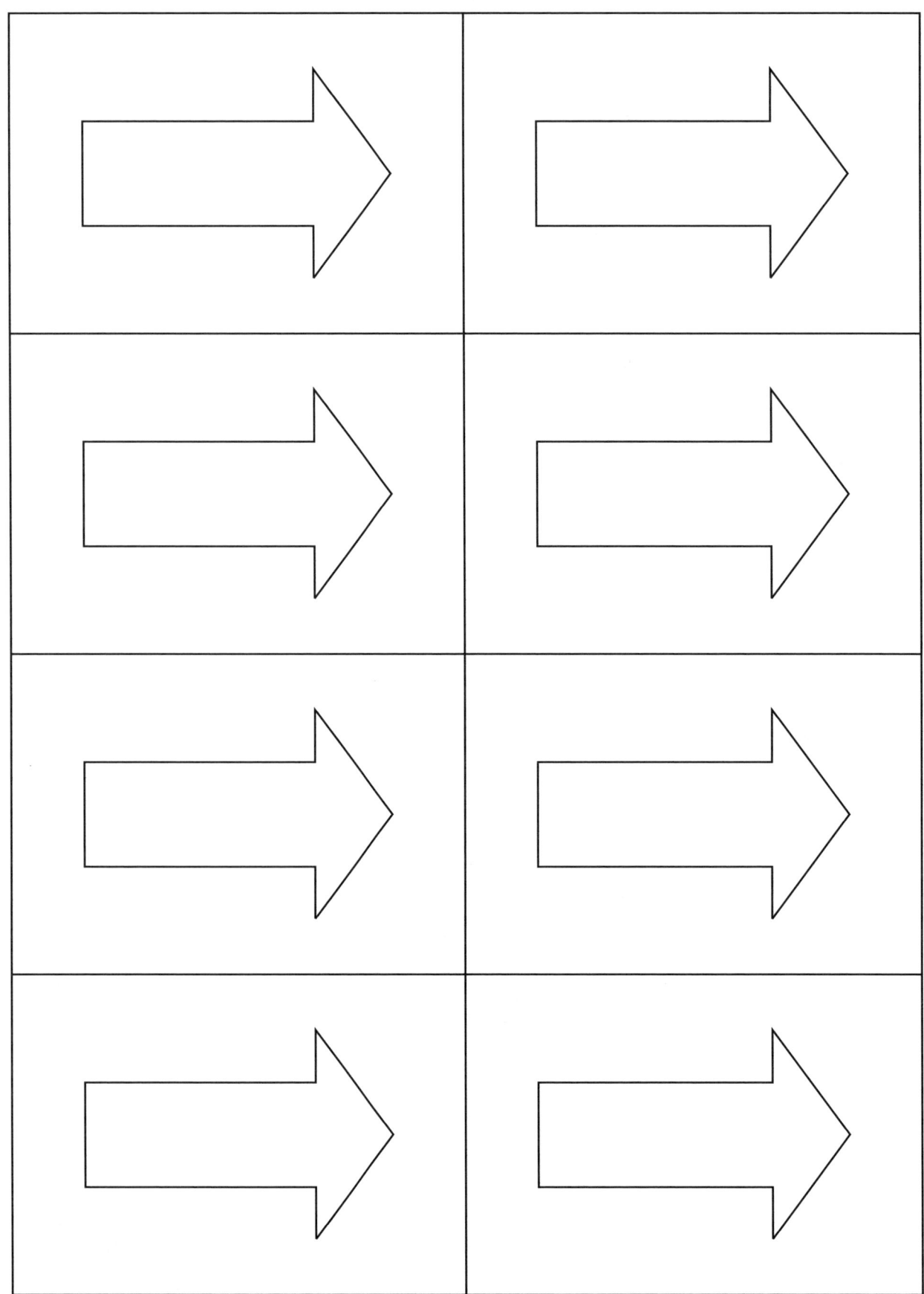

INTEGRATE IT!

Now take the following title and try it for yourself.

Pumpkin Jack
Written by Will Hubbell

Figure 6.3 *Pumpkin Jack* by Will Hubbell. Copyright © 2000 by Will Hubbell. Used by permission of Albert Whitman & Company.

When Tim carves his pumpkin for Halloween and names it Jack he never imagines the journey they would have together. During the winter months he watches as the pumpkin rots and becomes covered with snow in the garden. When spring arrives he covers Jack's remains with dirt and soon a sprout grows. He nurtures the plant and in the fall he is able to carve Jack again.

Pumpkin Jack

Tim names his carved pumpkin Jack. 	A candle makes Jack's face dance on the wall past the Halloween season. 
Tim takes the pumpkin to the garden to rot. 	Winter snow covers the moldy pumpkin. 

Pumpkin Jack

In the Spring a tiny sprout appears where Jack had been in the garden. 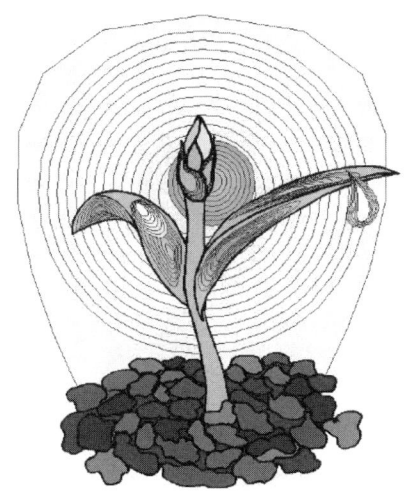	The sprout grows due to Tim's tender care. 
Flower blossoms appear on the vine. 	A little green ball ripens into a bright orange pumpkin. 

LINK IT!

Try linking some of these newly published titles to this reading strategy.

If You Take a Mouse to the Movies
Written by Laura Numeroff • Illustrated by Felicia Bond

Mouse loves going to the movies but doing so leads him to do other activities such as decorating Christmas trees, building snow forts, and singing holiday carols. The circular story line becomes complete after Mouse ends up requesting popcorn, which reminds him that he would like to go to the movies. (Although we are only highlighting two titles here, many of this author's books will work well with this strategy.)

If You Take a Mouse to School
Written by Laura Numeroff • Illustrated by Felicia Bond

Mouse is excited to be heading off to school. If you take him to school of course he will desire more including your lunchbox, some pencils, and recess time. The plot comes full circle when his requests led him back into the classroom.

This Is the Rain
Written by Lola M. Schaefer • Illustrated by Jane Wattenberg

Using rhyming text this cumulative tale explains the water cycle to young children. It describes each different step in the water cycle, including the role water vapor and evaporation plays in the process.

We're Going On a Lion Hunt
Written and illustrated by David Axtell

Two young girls travel through swishy swashy grass, a splishy splashy lake, and a big dark cave in hopes of finding a lion. Upon finally meeting a lion on the African savanna, they have to run back through the cave, lake, and grass to reach home. The story comes full circle when the girls begin to think about beginning the lion hunt again after a good night's sleep.

This Is the Sunflower
Written by Lola M. Schaefer • Illustrated by Donald Crews

The growing season of a sunflower is explored in this cumulative story. Readers discover the role birds, the earth, and the weather play in the creation of a garden of sunflowers.

And Then It Rained . . .
Written by Crescent Dragonwagon • Illustrated by Diane Greenseid

At first the people in the city enjoy the constant rain by participating in leisure activities like reading, baking bread and playing in puddles. Soon life becomes dull as the rain continues day after day. Brian makes wishes that the precipitation would stop. At this point in the story, readers can flip the book over and the read the companion tale—*And Then the Sun Came Out . . .* where everyone is enjoying the sun. Families are roller skating, taking strolls in the park, and enjoying ice cream. But too much of a good thing begins to make people in the city wish for rain thus starting the circular story again.

CHAPTER **seven**

Goal Structure Map

Language activities designed to help children understand story structure and develop story language are also designed to fill their backpacks with information necessary to comprehend the story.

The Power of Retelling, Benson and Cummins, 2000

KNOW IT!

A goal structure map can be a powerful retelling device. This graphic representation helps readers understand the connections between the important story units by looking at the main character's ultimate goal and the attempts he/she made to reach the goal. For each goal attempt a graphic representation shows the outcome of the attempt, whether it was successful or not. The goal structure map always ends with an examination of how the main character reacted to the ultimate outcome. It gives readers a chance to reflect on the feelings, thoughts, and actions of this character.

It is even possible to create goal structure maps for more than one character from a single story. The use of arrows can highlight connections and relationships between characters. In addition, arrows can show that one event caused or led to another event of a different character.

CREATE IT!

In a classroom with larger blocks of time, individual goal structure maps can be created by each student by using construction paper or sketching it on butcher paper. But given the time restraints of a library storytime, creating the pieces prior to the students arriving will save precious minutes. After creating and laminating the goal structure map pieces, the shapes become a tool to orally retell and revisit the story.

Using corresponding colored construction paper, create the appropriate number of shapes for the story. Next, text is written (or typed) and attached to shapes. Holes are punched in the top and bottom of each shape. Unbent paperclips can be used as hooks between shapes.

After reading the story, act as a facilitator and lead the whole group in a retelling of the story according to the attempts and outcomes of the main character. Begin with identifying the character's goal and hooking it with the unbent paperclip to the name of the character. Ask students to explain what the character first attempted to do to reach their goal. Have a child place this action on the goal structure map under the

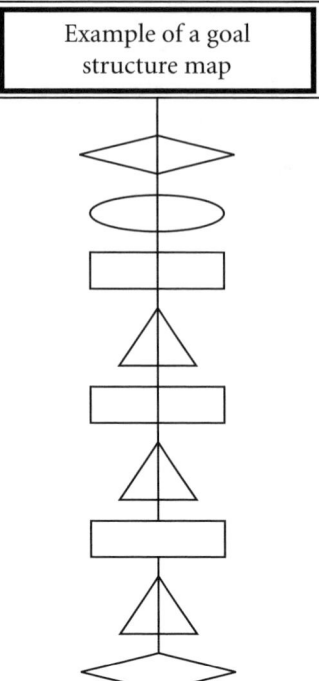

Figure 7.1 Example of chart.

goal. Students must identify the outcome of this action, attaching it. Continue retelling the story, building the chain as you go. The last item attached will identify the thoughts and feelings of the character after all the attempts and outcomes have been connected.

Goal Structure Map Key
Color and shape are kept uniform to help students understand the graphic representation.

Blue
Main character
Reaction/feelings/thoughts

Green
Attempts/Actions to reach goal

Purple
Character's goal

Orange
Outcome

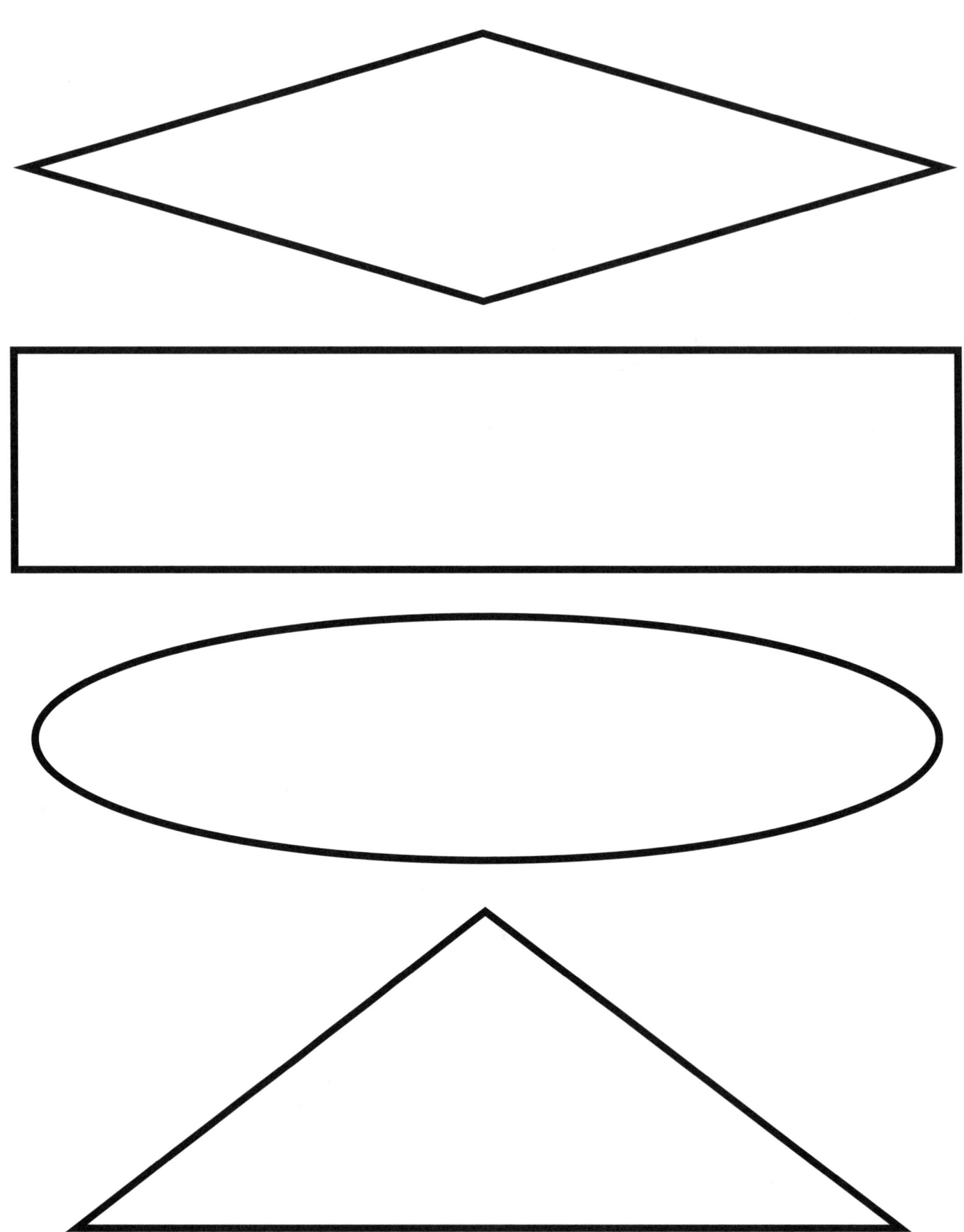

IMPLEMENT IT!

Now take the following *two* titles and try it for yourself.

Farmer McPeepers and His Missing Milk Cows
Written by Katy Duffield • Illustrated by Steve Gray

Figure 7.2 *Farmer McPeepers and His Missing Milk Cows* © 2003 by Katy Duffield. Illustrations © 2003 by Steve Gray. All rights reserved. Used by permission from Rising Moon.

A clever group of cows steal a pair of glasses from near-sighted Farmer McPeepers. As the poor farmer wanders through the town searching aimlessly for his missing cows, the herd of sneaky creatures are enjoying a day of swimming, baseball games, and movie-watching virtually under his unsuspecting nose.

Farmer McPeepers and His Missing Milk Cows

Farmer McPeepers

Wants to find his missing milk cows.

Farmer McPeepers checks the pond for his missing milk cows.

No
He doesn't see them!

Farmer McPeepers checks the swimming hole for his missing milk cows.

No

He doesn't see them!

Farmer McPeepers checks the playground for his missing milk cows.

No

He doesn't see them!

Farmer McPeepers checks outside the movie theater on the town square for his missing milk cows.

No

He doesn't see them!

Farmer McPeepers checks the school yard for his missing milk cows.

No

He doesn't see them!

Farmer McPeepers checks the ballpark's bleachers for his missing milk cows.

No

He doesn't see them!

Farmer McPeepers checks the barn dance for his missing milk cows.

No
He doesn't see them!

Farmer McPeepers returns to the barn and finds a something shining on the chopping block.

Yes!
He puts on his glasses and sees his missing milk cows.

Farmer McPeepers is relieved to know his missing milk cows are back in their places. (But for how long?)

Bringing Down the Moon
By Jonathan Emmett • Illustrated by Vanessa Cabban

Figure 7.3 *Bringing Down the Moon*. Text © 2001 by Jonathan Emmett. Illustrations © 2001 by Vanessa Cabban. Reproduced by permission of the publisher Candlewick Press, Inc., Cambridge, MA, on behalf of Walker Books Ltd., London.

Mole is so taken with the beauty of the moon that he attempts to grab it from the sky. He tries many different ways to reach it including jumping up high; poking it with a stick; throwing acorns at it; and climbing up to it, but he has little success. Eventually he learns to appreciate the moon in its home in the sky.

Bringing Down the Moon

Mole

Wants to have the moon for his very own.

Mole jumps up to pull the moon down.

No
It is not as close as it looks.

Mole gets a stick to poke the moon down.

No
It is not as close as it looks.

Mole throws acorns at the moon to knock it down.
No It is not as close as it looks.
Mole climbs the tree to carry the moon down.
No The moon's reflection is spotted in a puddle but it soon vanishes.
At first Mole is sad because he thinks he broke the moon. He soon realizes the moon went behind a cloud for a moment and it is still up in the sky. He admires its beauty.

LINK IT!

Try linking some of these newly published titles to this reading strategy.

Silly Little Goose
Written and illustrated by Nancy Tafuri

Goose wants to find an appropriate place to build a nest. First, she tries the pigs' pen because it is warm. Second, she tries to snuggle in with the kittens because it is soft. Next, Goose investigates building her nest with the sheep because it is quiet. She even tries to move into the cozy chicken coop. Finally, she finds a place that has all the elements of each place she has visited—warm, soft, quiet, and cozy. Goose lays her eggs in the perfect place—a hat!

Do Like a Duck Does
Written by Judy Hindley • Illustrated by Ivan Bates

Mama Duck has a new duckling waddling behind her. He looks like a fox but insists he is a big brown duck. Mama Duck thinks she knows the truth and a way to beat him at his own game. She is going to make him prove he is a duck by asking him to do things "like a duck does." She attempts to accomplish her goal by asking the Fox to eat worms, say quack, and jump in the river for a swim.

The Little Red Hen Makes a Pizza
Written by Philemon Sturges • Illustrated by Amy Walrod

The traditional folktale gets a new twist in this updated version. The Little Red Hen is making a delicious pizza. Her goal is to get her animal friends to help with the pizza making process. After numerous attempts to involve them, all of the outcomes are negative because they refuse to do anything. The ending has a unique twist when the Little Red Hen ends up making a huge pizza. Because of the sheer size of her creation, she decides to share it with the other animals. In response to this kind gesture, the animals decide to finally help by cleaning up after dinner.

Bedhead
By Margie Palatini • Illustrated by Jack E. Davis

As Oliver gets out of bed one morning he looks into the mirror and notices he has a terrific case of "bedhead." His family tries everything to help him tame the unruly mess but nothing seems to work. Finally with a baseball hat firmly planted on his head, they think the problem is solved. Unfortunately, Oliver gets to school and finds that it is school picture day and all hats must be removed!

The Dirty Little Boy
Written by Margaret Wise Brown • Illustrated by Steven Salerno

The dirty little boy wants to get clean after getting jam, chocolate, and mud all over himself. He asks his mother for help bathing but she is too busy and tells him to run along and see how the animals take their baths. He watches the bird, pig, cat, and horse and tries to copy their bathing techniques with disastrous results. Mom then scoops him up and shows him how to take a nice soapy bath. In the end he is squeaky clean.

Hedgie's Surprise
Written and illustrated by Jan Brett

Every morning Tomten raids Henny's nest for her egg. He doesn't like the porridge that is made for him to eat so he steals and eats the egg instead. Henny hates losing her egg because she wants to continue sitting on it so she can have chicks. So working with Hedgie the hedgehog, Henny tries to trick Tomten. They try to prevent him from stealing the egg by substituting an acorn, a strawberry, a mushroom, and a potato in the nest. When nothing seems to work to stop Tomten, Hedgie surprises him with a handful of needles in her nest. Henny never has to worry again!

Muncha Muncha Muncha
Written by Candace Fleming • Illustrated by G. Brian Karas

Mr. McGreeley plants a wonderful garden full of delicious vegetables. Unfortunately those vegetables are the favorites of the three bunnies who keep watch over his garden. Mr. McGreeley is determined to keep the bunnies out. He builds a series of things to keep the bunnies at bay including a small wire fence, a tall wooden wall, a deep wet trench, and a huge enormous "thing." Eventually the bunnies get in by hiding in his basket.

Rattletrap Car
Written by Phyllis Root • Illustrated by Jill Barton

It's a hot summer's day and the family wants to go to the lake but they are unsure if they will make it in their rattletrap car. The kids pack the car with toys, razzleberry fizz soda, and some chocolate marshmallow fudge delight ice cream. On the journey the car breaks down a number of times, but luckily the family is able to fix the car each time and get to the lake by using the items they packed. This book has wonderful words to help with the sound effects.

Stella Louella's Runaway Book
Written and illustrated by Lisa Campbell Ernst

Stella Louella's library book is missing and the whole town joins in to help her find it. Many townspeople have seen the book but they have all passed it on to another interested reader. Now the whole group must head into the library to tell Mrs. Graham, the librarian, the book is lost. Little do they know that Mrs. Graham found the book on the bench outside the library.

Tub-Boo-Boo
By Margie Palatini • Illustrated by Glin Dibley

While taking a bath Henry gets his big toe caught in the spigot when trying to stop a drip from dropping. Now he is stuck in the bath and everyone who comes in to help makes a "tub-boo-boo" and gets stuck as well. After Mom, Dad, and the policeman are all stuck they finally call a plumber. He helps a little but nothing gets them all loose until know-it-all big sister Lucy comes in with her ice cream cone and sets them all free with a few slick well-paced droplets.

CHAPTER

Story Element Map

To understand story structure, children must be able to identify the literary elements in the story—in other words, the components that stories have in common. These are the elements that children who have been read to at home have come to sense intuitively: setting, plot, character, theme, point of view, style. These elements give story its structure.

Power of Retelling, Benson and Cummins, 2000

KNOW IT!

A story element map describes the structure of a story by identifying the elements that make up the text: characters, setting, problem, and solution. Creating a map helps students develop summarization skills and a sense of story. It helps readers focus their thinking on the important elements of a story, not the unimportant details. Maps can range from simple to very complex. Because primary students are our focus audience, the story element maps illustrated in this text are very simplistic. Additional elements could be added to increase complexity, for example, events, theme, beginning, middle, end, conflict, and climax.

CREATE IT!

A story element map is a quick and painless way to summarize a story. Ideally students generate elements that an educator writes on the chart. But in the confines of a short library time, this becomes unrealistic. A reusable template can be created to name and sort elements. First, use a large piece of poster board and attach the different categories on the chart: STORY ELEMENT MAP; CHARACTERS; SETTING; AUTHOR; TITLE; PROBLEM; and SOLUTION. Next, pre-read the story and type up the elements specific to the book. Be sure to laminate the story element map and the pre-printed elements.

If the story is relatively short, this graphic organizer can be done in one session. First, share the story with students. Ask them to be listening for the story elements to be added to the chart later. After the story is complete, ask for volunteers to identify the author, title, characters, setting, problem, and solution. After each element is identified a volunteer can come up to the story element map and use tacky adhesive to attach the pre-made elements in the proper place.

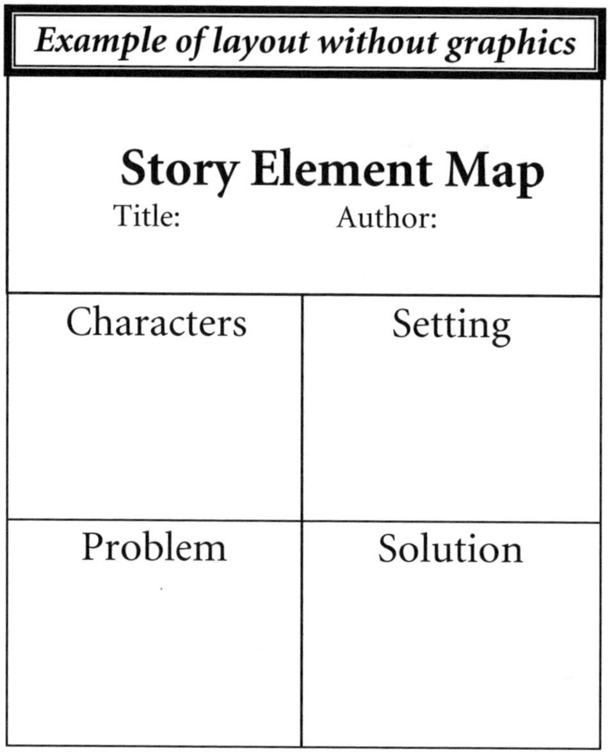

> *Example of layout without graphics*
>
> **Story Element Map**
> Title: Author:
>
> | Characters | Setting |
> |---|---|
> | Problem | Solution |

Figure 8.1 Example of chart.

A story element map can also be used as a review tool a week after a story is read. This is especially effective if students are participating in a genre or author study. Completing the story element map serves as a quick reminder of what happened last week.

Story Element Map

Title:

Author:

Setting

Characters

Problem

Solution

INTEGRATE IT!

Now take the following *three* titles and try if for yourself.

Just Ducky
Written and illustrated by Kathy Mallat

Figure 8.2 *Just Ducky* Copyright 2002 © Kathy Mallat. Published by Walker & Company.

Ducky is looking for a playmate. He asks the bee, the mouse, and the frog to play, but they are all busy. As Ducky begins to feel sad because of his predicament, he looks down towards the pond and discovers someone that wants to play. He never knew he could have quite so much fun with his own reflection.

Just Ducky

Written and Illustrated by Kathy Mallat

Ducky

Mama

Bee

Mouse

Frog

It's a beautiful day at the pond.

Ducky can't find anyone to play with.

He looks into the water and plays with his reflection.

Dirt Boy
Written by Erik Jon Slangerup • Illustrated by John Manders

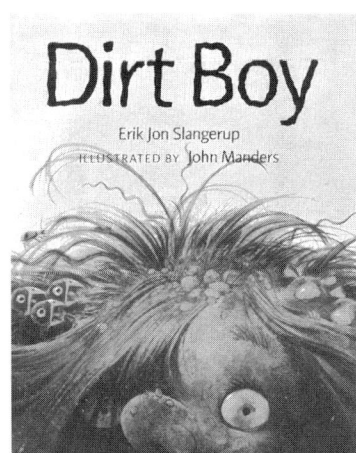

Figure 8.3 *Dirt Boy* by Erik Jon Slangerup, illustrated by John Manders. Text © 2000 by John Manders. Cover reprinted by permission of Albert Whitman & Company.

Fister Farnello hates taking a bath. In fact he dislikes baths so much he runs away from home to avoid taking one. In the woods he becomes friends with a filthy giant named Dirt Man. Fister enjoys his new disgusting life until moss starts to creep out of his bellybutton and he starts crying big muddy tears. Will his mother even recognize her little boy?

Dirt Boy

Written by Erik Jon Slangerup

Fister
Farnello
Dirt Boy

Mother

Dirt Man

Woods

Fister loves dirt and hates baths.

He runs away to the forest where he lives with Dirt Man. Soon moss starts to creep out of his bellybutton and purple mushrooms pop out between his toes. After the Dirt Man tries to eat Fister, the dirt boy runs home and begins to bathe.

My Friend Rabbit
Written and illustrated by Eric Rohmann

Although Rabbit has the best of intentions, trouble always seems to follow him. When he accidentally gets Mouse's airplane stuck in a tree, Rabbit tries to retrieve the airplane by stacking all of the animals he can find into a tall pyramid. But the well-meaning Rabbit runs into more trouble when his reluctant pyramid of friends topples over.

My Friend Rabbit

Written and Illustrated by Eric Rohmann

Rabbit	Elephant
Crocodile	Squirrel

Bear	Duck	Mouse

Baby ducks

| Hippo | Rhino |
| Deer | Forest |

Rabbit throws the airplane that belongs to Mouse up into a tree so high he can't get it down.

Rabbit has a plan to stack all of his animal friends on top of each other so they can reach the top of the tree and get the airplane. The animals fall, but Mouse gets his plane down. In the end, the plane flies up into the treetop, getting stuck again.

LINK IT!

Try linking some of these newly published titles to this reading strategy.

Car Wash
Written by Sandra and Susan Steen • Illustrated by G. Brian Karas

This clever story is told from the perspective of two young children who use their imagination while watching everything happen to their vehicle during a car wash. Their car becomes a submarine bouncing on the foamy sea narrowly avoiding an accident with an octopus. From the portholes (windows) they can see the approaching hurricane!

Close Your Eyes
Written by Kate Banks • Illustrated by Georg Hallensleben

Little Tiger needs to take a nap but is scared to close his eyes. His mother discusses all of the wonderful and magical things he will see in his dreams. In addition, she reassures him that she will be here for Little Tiger when he wakes up.

The Rain Came Down
Written and illustrated by David Shannon

When the first raindrop comes down it starts a chain of events that effects the whole town: the chickens squawk, which excites a cat, which makes a dog bark, which makes a man yell, which wakes up a baby, etc. Soon everyone in town is fussing with each other in grouchy language. Then as quickly as it began, the rain stops and the sun peeks out. Moods lighten up and the townspeople stop arguing and begin to forgive each other for the things they had said or done . . . when the rain came down.

Book! Book! Book!
Written by Deborah Bruss • Illustrated by Tiphanie Beeke

The farm animals are bored on the farm so they decide to head to the public library to find some interesting books to read. The confused librarian has a hard time figuring out what the horse, goat, cow, and pig are trying to say. Finally, when the hen clucks "Book! Book! BOOK!" the librarian understands and gives them books to read. The animals head back to the farm excited about their new books, . . . except the literary minded bullfrog. He already "Read-it, read-it, READ-it!"

Farmer Brown Goes Round and Round
Written by Teri Sloat • Illustrated by Nadine Bernard Westcott

A tornado touches down and creates chaos on Farmer Brown's farm. The animals get their sounds mixed up causing the pigs to moo, the sheep to cluck, and the goats to meow. Will it take another natural disaster to return Farmer Brown's twisted farm back to normal?

Click, Clack, Moo Cows That Type
Written by Doreen Cronin • Illustrated by Betsy Lewin

Farmer Brown has a problem. His cows have possession of a typewriter and are demanding electric blankets. When Farmer Brown says "No" the cows revolt and explain in a letter that if they do not receive blankets then there will be no milk. Next, the hens become involved deciding they too want blankets or no eggs will be produced. Farmer Brown is furious with the farmyard boycott, but with the negotiating skills of the ducks an agreement is reached. Finally Farmer Brown's problems are solved . . . .or are they?

Farm Flu
Written by Teresa Bateman • Illustrated by Nadine Bernard Westcott

After mother heads out of town, a young boy is forced to take care of the farm animals on his own. The cow gets sick with the flu so the young man decides to care for the animal the way his mom would take care of him if he was ill. He tucks the cow into bed and brings him soothing tea. Soon all the animals are getting sick and the boy has trouble finding room for them all in the house!

Swollobog
Written and illustrated by Alastair Taylor

Swollobog is a silly dog that swallows everything she can get in her mouth. She is constantly begging for food. When she takes a trip to the fair with her family, Swollobog's obsession with eating causes big problems and sends the family on an adventure they will never forget.

Queenie Farmer Had Fifteen Daughters
Written by Ann Campbell • Illustrated by Holly Meade

Queenie Farmer is a busy lady tending to her herd of fifteen daughters. Between cooking for them, sewing their clothes, and finding them husbands she hardly has a moment to rest all week long. When her grown-up herd of daughters have a total of fifty-five grandbabies, Queenie spends all week long building buggies, knitting booties, and quilting comforters. But after a deliberate move to the country, Queenie begins to spend just Sundays with the grandbabies, changing their diapers, singing them to sleep, and kissing them good-bye. The rest of the week she spends doing whatever she chooses.

The Smushy Bus
Written by Leslie Helakoski • Illustrated by Salvatore Murdocca

Mr. Mathers, the school bus driver, is running late to pick the kids up from Addington School. When he finally arrives he has only a little bus with four seats. Mr. Mathers realizes he has quite a problem because 76 kids are waiting to go home. Using his problem-solving skills, he divides and groups the kids to fit them on the bus. Does his mathematical reasoning see him through? Will he have any more problems for the "remainder" of the day?

The Name Quilt
Written by Phyllis Root • Illustrated by Margot Apple

Grandma has a special family heirloom that tells the story of Sadie's family. Sadie could spend hours listening to Grandma relate the adventure attached with each scrap of fabric. One summer day a storm blows the quilt away, frightening Sadie into believing that all the special memories are gone. Luckily Grandma and Sadie hold the family history in their hearts.

Compare and Contrast

CHAPTER nine

T-Table

Some struggling readers have difficulty organizing a mass of new information into categories and relationships. Instead of trying to remember every new fact as an unrelated piece of information, these students need help organizing the new information into categories and relating it their background knowledge.

Supporting Struggling Readers, Walker, 1992

KNOW IT!

A T-table is an excellent graphic organizer to use to sort and categorize information from a story. Using a T-table gives primary children a hands-on device to manipulative language. It can be used to sort words and phrases in an infinite number of ways, for example, fact/opinion; real/imaginary; yes/no; summer/winter. The versatility of this graphic organizer is its best feature. It can be manipulated to fit the needs of a wide variety of stories where matching or categorizing is desired. This is helpful as students are asked to make sense of information they have received from a text. A T-table asks them to organize this information in a systematic way.

CREATE IT!

Using a piece of poster board draw the large T design with magic marker. After pre-reading a story that is suited to sorting, type up appropriate words and phrases. Laminate the reusable T-table template and the word/phrase sheet. Cut apart the phrases for sorting. If you are using the activity with Kindergarten students, clip art may be used in place of some phrases to help aid in comprehension.

Before reading the story to students explain what they will be doing with the T-table. This preparatory step sets a reason for reading. After the story has been shared, begin sorting the phrases. Read each phrase aloud and ask for a volunteer to indicate where it belongs on the chart. The phrases can be attached to the appropriate place using tacky adhesive. If the activity is more of a matching game, place one-half of the phrase slips on one side of the board. Ask helpers to come up and match the second half with its partner.

Figure 9.1 Example of chart.

INTEGRATE IT!

Now take the following *two* titles and try it for yourself.

Leaving Home
Written by Sneed B. Collard III • Illustrated by Joan Dunning

Figure 9.2 *Leaving Home* by Sneed B. Collard, illustrated by Joan Dunning. Jacket art copyright © 2002 by Joan Dunning. Reprinted by permission of Houghton Mifflin Company. All rights reserved.

Flying lizards can glide. Crabs can crawl. This text explains how animals move in unique ways depending on their body construction. A T-table could be used with young children to match animals with their corresponding way of moving.

Leaving Home

Written by Sneed B. Collard III
Illustrated by Joan Dunning

Animal

Movement

hawk	fly
shark	swim
rabbit	hop
flying lizard	glide
frog	hop

rhinoceros	snake	whale	butterfly	jaguar	crab
walk	crawl	swim	fly	walk	crawl

In November
Written by Cynthia Rylant • Illustrated by Jill Kastner

Figure 9.3 *In November* by Cynthia Rylant, illustrated by Jill Kastner. Copyright © 2000. Reprinted by permission of Harcourt Publishing.

Beautiful oil paintings illustrate the autumn activities and traditions associated with the month of November. People and tiny creatures prepare for winter in many ways; seeking shelter, gathering food, and counting their blessings. Learners could use a T-table to sort activities traditionally associated with November from those connected with May.

In November

Written by Cynthia Rylant

November

May

The earth is growing quiet.

Life is hiding beneath a blanket of white.

The trees are still.

Some birds are leaving to go on a long journey.
The air is full of good-byes.
The air is chilly.
Mice pile under logs.
Bees pile up in earthy holes.
Dogs lie before fireplaces.

People sip cider and give thanks.
People give presents, hugs, and cards to their mothers.
Birds are returning from long journeys.
The air is filled with spring chirping.
The earth is alive with new plants sprouting.

Trees are budding with new life.
The air is warm.
Mice run about in the meadow.
Dogs and cats explore the outdoors.
People begin to swim and picnic.
Bees find new blossoms to visit.

LINK IT!

Try linking these newly published titles to this reading strategy.

Good Thing You're Not an Octopus!
Written by Julie Markes • Illustrated by Maggie Smith

As a little boy goes through the routine activities that make up his day he thinks about how different it would be to do these activities if he were an animal. For example, getting dressed would be much harder if you were an octopus because you would have so many arms to fit in the proper places. After reflecting on bathtime, naptime, and mealtime the boy realizes that the best thing to be is himself. A T-table chart could be used to match the animal with the difficult task.

Snow
Written and illustrated by Manya Stojic

Moose, bear, fox and other creatures prepare for winter. Using simple text this beautifully illustrated story shows all of the rituals animals participate in as the snow begins to fall. As winter approaches the bear prepares for sleep; the geese fly south; and the rabbit's fur begins to turn white. A T-table could be used to sort activities from two different seasons.

Now What Can I Do?
Written by Margaret Park Bridges • Illustrated by Melissa Sweet

Little Raccoon does not want to do his chores on this rainy day. With Mommy's help Little Raccoon finds out how even chores can be fun. On facing pages, readers see the chore and how Little Raccoon imagines it to be in his head. For example, picking up the clothes on the floor becomes an archaeological dig for the fossil remains of a sock. A T-table could be used to match Little Raccoon's chore with his imaginative adventure.

The Cat Barked?
Written and illustrated by Lydia Monks

A cat imagines her life would be better if she was a dog. After all, dogs do seem to have all the fun—going to the park, guarding the houses, and being the heroes in stories. The cat's owner points out that if she were a dog she would have to do some things she wouldn't enjoy like eating bones, being on a leash, and fetching sticks. The cat is finally convinced she is happy to be a cat. An eavesdropping dog now begins to question his species at the end. Using a T-table, learners could sort activities listed in the text into two categories: cat activities/dog activities.

Two Little Trains
Written by Margaret Wise Brown • Illustrated by Leo and Diane Dillon

Two little trains are traveling west. One train is a fast-moving streamlined steam engine. The other one is a slow-moving old-fashioned toy train. Although these two means of transportation don't seem to have much in common, a little imagination brings the two worlds together. On opposite pages readers follow the trains across bridges, over rivers, and through tunnels. A T-table could be used to compare and contrast the different journeys each train takes.

Why Do Kittens Purr?
Written by Marion Dane Bauer • Illustrated by Henry Cole

This story explains why animals behave the way they do. It discusses why kittens purr, why spiders spin webs, and why mice squeak. Various other animal habits and behaviors are explored through rhyming text. A T-table could be used to match an animal with its behavior.

Hello, Hello!
Written by Miriam Schlein • Illustrated by Daniel Kirk

How do animals say "Hello"? Elephants twine their trunks together. Chimpanzees touch hands, hug, or kiss. Beavers touch noses. This book explores how animals greet each other in different ways. A T-table could be used to match the form of animal communication with the correct animal species.

Hondo & Fabian
Written and illustrated by Peter McCarty

Hondo the dog and Fabian the cat are best friends who usually spend every day and night together. Today these two creatures will have very different adventures. Hondo will spend the day playing in the waves at the beach. Fabian will spend the day diving for the door as the baby chases her. A T-table could be used to sort the different activities according to the participant, Hondo or Fabian.

The Pie Is Cherry
Written and illustrated by Michael Rex

"The timer is ringing. The cereal is colorful." Come through the kitchen during mealtime and experience all of the interesting sights, smells, sounds, and tastes. Sentences from the story could be sorted by sense (touch, sight, sound, smell, and taste) on a modified T-table.

Kate and the Beanstalk
Written by Mary Pope Osborne • Illustrated by Giselle Potter

In this twisted fairy tale, Kate uses her clever wit to outsmart the giant and claim a fortune for her family. Characteristics of fairy tales, (such as goodness wins over evil; make-believe characters; wishes are granted) could be sorted on a T-table. Label one column "Yes" and one "No." Learners indicate whether this characteristic is in the story (Yes) or it is missing from the text (No).

You Forgot Your Skirt, Amelia Bloomer
Written by Shana Corey • Illustrated by Chesley McLauren

This is a true story about a very improper woman who lived in the early 1800s. Amelia Bloomer thought proper ladies were silly. She believed that women should have the right to vote, to work, and to wear clothing that would allow them to move about with ease. To solve her clothing concern, she designed special pants that would allow women to participate in activities that were difficult to do because of the restrains of the long dresses women were suppose to wear at the time. Amelia's designs became very popular and were called "bloomers." A T-table could be used to sort facts from the story from the opinions people possessed in the 1800s.

CHAPTER

Venn Diagram

As readers compare and contrast, then summarize or distill information from a variety of sources, they must synthesize information and integrate new knowledge into their existing knowledge base.

Teaching for Comprehension in Reading K-2, DeFord, 2003

KNOW IT!

A Venn Diagram provides readers with the opportunity to compare and contrast characteristics of stories in a very visual way. By using two intersecting circles to sort elements of different texts, the reader brings abstract ideas into a concrete realm. These graphic organizers can be used to reflect on the similarities and differences between two stories regarding plot lines, characters, settings, and thematic elements. Asking students to make comparisons requires them to infer and draw conclusions about what happened in the story, an important skills we want to cultivate in our young readers. Using a Venn Diagram is especially effective when comparing two different versions of the same story.

CREATE IT!

Although physically writing information that students generate on a Venn Diagram is the most ideal way of creating this graphic organizer; it isn't realistic in a library storytime because the task is time consuming. Having events, characters, and thematic elements pre-printed on laminated slips of paper will save some time. Create and laminate a template of two intersecting circles that you can use multiple times with many stories. Next, print and laminate story characteristics on slips of paper. Tacky adhesive can be used to attach and reattach these phrases when necessary. Another option is to draw the Venn Diagram on chart paper that will be given away to a student after it is created. Story characteristics can be printed on adhesive sticky labels. As elements are sorted, students can "stick" them in the correct section of the Venn Diagram.

Because two stories will need to be shared in order to create a Venn Diagram, a minimum of two sessions is required for this activity. If both stories are lengthy, three sessions may be necessary. For example, two sessions will be needed to share each of the respective stories. An additional session will be needed to picture-walk back through the two texts so the stories are fresh in the minds of students. After walking back through each text briefly retelling the story by only using the illustrations, students can begin to sort different characteristics on the chart.

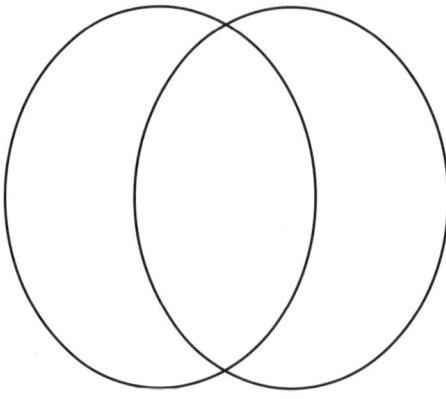

Venn Diagram

Figure 10.1 Example of chart.

INTEGRATE IT!

Now take the following titles and try it for yourself.

The Three Pigs
Written and illustrated by David Wiesner

Figure 10.2 *The Three Pigs* by David Wiesner. Jacket illustration copyright © 2001 by David Wiesner. Reprinted by permission of Clarion Books/Houghton Mifflin Company. All rights reserved.

In this unique version of *The Three Little Pigs*, the main characters are escaping from their story and beginning to run around in other tales. During their travels, they meet other characters including a fairytale dragon, a cat with a fiddle, and the cow that jumped over the moon. After wondering which story to stay in, the pigs decide their own book is worth revisiting. With the help of their new friends this story ends much differently than the original version.

Compare it with . . .

Wait No Paint!
Written and illustrated by Bruce Whatley

In the twisted take on *The Three Little Pigs*, the main characters are on their usual quest to outsmart the wolf. A mysterious voice, the book's illustrator, declares that he is running out of red paint and can no longer paint the pigs pink. After many silly attempts to correct the problem with a variety of other methods, the pigs decide they can't take the stress any longer so they inform the illustrator that they don't want to be in the story anymore. The illustrator fixes the problem in a most creative fashion.

Three Pigs/Wait! No Paint!
The pigs make three different houses out of a variety of materials.
The author has twisted a folk tale.
One of the pigs is made to look like a clown.
The main characters are pigs.
A fairy tale dragon and a nursery rhyme cat help solve the problem in the story.
The wolf is tricked.
The illustrator runs out of red paint.

The end of the story is different from the original version.
The characters leave the story and enter another one.
A slamming door hurts the wolf's nose.
The pigs use the pages of the story as a paper airplane.
The main characters explore the world outside of the *The Three Little Pig* tale.
The pigs get blown out of the story.
A mysterious person spills juice on the story.

The Princess and the Pizza
Written by Mary Jane Auch • Illustrated by Herm Auch

Figure 10.3 *The Princess and the Pizza* © 2002 by Mary Jane and Herm Auch. Reproduced by permission of publisher Holiday House.

Prince Drupert is looking for a bride who needs to have all the qualities of a true princess. Paulina thinks she could be a perfect match, but first she has to beat out the competition. Eleven other princesses from miles around have come to prove how "princess-like" they can be. After participating in a variety of crazy tests, the final competition becomes a cooking contest in this twisted fairy tale.

Compare it with . . .

The Princess and the Pea
Adapted and Illustrated by Alain Vaes

Prince Ralph wants to get married but his selfish mother has her own reasons for not wanting him to wed. The Queen agrees to let Prince Ralph marry but only after the applicants pass her silly tests that involve performing yo-yo tricks and playing hopscotch blindfolded. Prince Ralph stumbles upon one potential candidate that is not only beautiful and smart but handy too. Opal, a tow-truck driving princess is up for the Queen's series of wedding challenges.

Princess and the Pizza/Princess and the Pea
The princess applicants have to do silly tasks like play hopscotch, spin yo-yos, and complete string tricks to be considered for marriage.
One potential bride drives a tow truck and can fix cars.
The author twisted the classic fairy tale version in a unique way.
The Princess has to sleep on a stack of mattresses with a pea under one.
The princess needs a job.
The chosen princess decides she has other plans and doesn't need to marry a prince.

The prince finds a suitable princess and marries her.

The princess must be able answer joke questions to be worthy of the Prince's love.

The Queen makes the potential brides perform numerous silly tests.

The winning candidate is fairly handy and independent.

The princesses have to prove their cooking skills by preparing a feast.

Characters from other fairy tales appear in the story.

LINK IT!

Try linking some of these newly published titles to this reading strategy.

One Monday
Written and illustrated by Amy Huntington

One Monday the wind blew so hard it straightened the pigs' curly tails. It continued every day of that week to blow and cause havoc on Annabelle's farm. Finally it was Sunday and the wind blew right on out of town. The next week brings on a new weather predicament.

Compare it with . . .

The Wind Blew
Written and illustrated by Pat Hutchins

When the wind blows it picks up different items and carries them in the air. It sweeps up numerous items including an umbrella, hat, balloon and a kite, keeping them away from their owners. Finally, the wind quiets down, dropping all the stolen items and blowing out to sea.

Too Many Monsters
Written by Eve Bunting • Illustrated by James Bernardin

As a little boy is trying to go to sleep he sees a number of monsters in his room. There are monsters reading books, painting toenails, and even eating popcorn under his bed. His family works together to come up with a great solution to help get rid of the monsters.

Compare it with . . .

There's a Nightmare in my Closet
Written and illustrated by Mercer Mayer

There's a unwanted nightmare in a young boy's closet so he decides to get rid of it. One night the boy waits up and quickly turns on his light to catch the monster as it creeps out of the closet. His nightmare begins to cry uncontrollably. The boy befriends the nightmare, offering a place in his bed to sleep.

Sometimes I'm Bombaloo
Written by Rachel Vail • Illustrated by Yumi Heo

Katie Honors is a very nice little girl. She follows directions and always uses the magic word. Until she gets angry . . . then she is "bombaloo." During these times she has trouble controlling herself and can do things that she is not proud of. After spending some time alone she regains her control and is able to play nicely with others again.

Compare it with . . .

When Sophie Gets Angry—Really, Really Angry . . .
Written and illustrated by Molly Bang

How does Sophie deal with her anger? When a toy snatched is taken away from her it takes climbing a tree in Sophie's special place to calm her down. The vibrant illustrations help show how her mood changes as her anger subsides.

Oliver Finds His Way
Written by Phyllis Root • Illustrated by Christopher Denise

Oliver plays outside while his parents are busy working around the yard. He spots a yellow leaf and follows it to the edge of the forest. When he finally looks up he doesn't see his house or the lovely leaf. Oliver begins to realize he doesn't know the way home.

Compare it with . . .

Quack, Daisy, Quack!
Written and illustrated by Jane Simmons

Mama has taken Daisy and Pip to visit Aunt Lily. These baby ducks have found the perfect spot to engage in loud playtime activities—the feeding pond. They become so excited they lose their Mama. How will they ever find their way back to their Mama?

The Flea's Sneeze
Written by Lynn Downey • Illustrated by Karla Firehammer

All the animals are asleep in the barn and no one hears the flea who is about to sneeze. When he sneezes it begins a chain reaction with the other animals in the barn. They begin to wake up, making noise. Someone hands the flea a tissue and they all settle back down to go back to sleep, except the sniffling hog.

Compare it with . . .

The Napping House
Written by Audrey Wood • Illustrated by Don Wood

In this house a granny, child, dog, cat, mouse and flea are enjoying a serene slumber all piled in the same bed. In this cumulative rhyming story, the flea causes quite a commotion as it begins to wake up on top of the pile of sleeping creatures.

Cindy Ellen: A Wild Western Cinderella
Written by Susan Lowell • Illustrated by Jane Manning

In this western spin of the story of *Cinderella*, Cindy Ellen is a sweet cowgirl who helps around the ranch and takes care of her nasty stepsisters. With the help of a fast-talking fairy godmother, Cindy Ellen is able to win the heart of Joe Prince, the rodeo champion. After twirling at the square dance with Joe, Cindy Ellen runs off leaving a diamond spur behind.

Compare it with . . .

Joe Cinders
Written by Marianne Mitchell • Illustrated by Bryan Langdo

In this southwestern gender twisting *Cinderella*, Joe Cinders lives on a ranch with his three stepbrothers who make him do all the chores. One day Rosalinda invites them to a fiesta because she is scouting for a husband. Luckily a mysterious fellow in overalls and a serape visits Joe and helps him become presentable for Rosalinda. He gives Joe a pair of brand-new jeans, a white sombrero, red boots, and a shiny pickup truck to drive to the fiesta.

Dusty Locks and The Three Bears
Written by Susan Lowell • Illustrated by Randy Cecil

This is the tale of *Goldilocks and the Three Bears* with a western spin. Dusty Locks is a dirty little girl who has no problems breaking into the Grizzlies' home. As she makes herself comfortable in the vacant cabin, she finds plates of beans to sample. Following the traditional tale, Dusty Locks eventually is discovered when the Grizzlies arrive home.

Compare it with . . .

Goldilocks Returns
Written and illustrated by Lisa Campbell Ernst

Fifty years later Goldilocks is still haunted by her trip to the Bears' residence. She feels guilty for what she did as a child so she goes back to redeem herself. She reinforces the locks on the doors, stocks the cabinets with healthy foods, and redecorates the house with new curtains and pillows. Will the Bear family appreciate her efforts?

Earthquack!
Written by Margie Palatini • Illustrated by Barry Moser

In the spirit of the folktale *Henny-Penny*, Chucky Lucky believes the rumbling in the meadow to be the earth quaking. He proceeds to inform all the barnyard animals of his fears. The Wily Weasel is about to take advantage of the hysteria when the true source of the grumbling is revealed.

Compare it with . . .

Henny-Penny
Retold by Jane Wattenberg

In this retelling of the traditional folktale, photographs of friendly fowls illustrate the story of *Henny-Penny*. The hysterical hen is sure that the sky is falling when an acorn hits her on the head. As she rushes off to inform the king, she runs into many friends who join her in her quest. They run into a hungry fox who tries to trick them into visiting his dark cave so he can have a delicious bird feast.

Comprehension

CHAPTER

Q.A.R. (Question–Answer Relationship)

An important part of helping children develop the strategy of questioning involves helping them consider where the answers to their questions might be found.

Comprehension: Strategic Instruction for K-3 Students, Owocki, 2003

KNOW IT!

Q.A.R., Question–Answer Relationship, is a strategy students can use to increase their success answering comprehension questions (Raphael, 1984). It is most appropriate to use with students in second grade and up. This strategy gives readers a systematic way of analyzing the task demands of different types of questions. It requires students to decide what type of question is being asked, thereby indicating where to go to get the information needed to answer it. There are four categories for Q.A.R. questions to be sorted into: *Right There*; *Think and Search*; *Author and You*; and *On Your Own*. A *Right There* question is one where the answer is in the text, usually easy to find. A *Think and Search* question is one where the answer is in the story, but the reader needs to put together different parts to answer it. An *Author and You* question is one where the answer is NOT in the story. The reader needs to think about what he/she already knows, what the author tells them, and how it connects. An *On Your Own* question is another one where the answer is NOT in the story. The reader can answer the question without reading the story.

CREATE IT!

A large reusable chart can be used to help students sort questions from the text into the Q.A.R. categories. Using a piece of poster board, place one of each of the four Q.A.R. strategies in each of the corners. In the center place the Q.A.R. QUESTION–ANSWER RELATIONSHIP; TITLE; and AUTHOR text headings. Pre-read the text and generate a set of comprehension questions to ask students. Try to create at least two questions for each of the four Q.A.R. categories. After typing these questions up, laminate the questions and the poster board. Cut the questions into slips for students to sort.

Before sharing the story with students, introduce the different Q.A.R. categories. Explain that this strategy will help them know where to go to find answers to questions. Attaching an action to each category will help some students connect with the strategies. To indicate a *Right There* question students may pretend they are holding an open book with their hands. A *Think and Search* question might be indicated by

Example of layout without graphics		
Right There		Think and Search
Title:	**Q.A.R.** Question-Answer Relationship	Author:
Author and You		On Your Own

Figure 11.1 Example of chart.

flapping the open book with their hands. To show that a question is an *Author and You*, students might place their pretend book on top of their heads to show that it takes their brain and the author's words to find the answer. An *On Your Own* question might be indicated with the children pointing to themselves.

After learning about the four categories, share the story with students. Afterwards read a comprehension question and have the entire group show with the appropriate action what Q.A.R. category the question belongs in. Ask a volunteer to come use tacky adhesive to stick it to the correct corner and answer the question for the group.

Q.A.R.
Question-Answer Relationship

Author:

Title:

Right There

You can find the answer *right there* in the story.

Think and Search

You can find the answer in the story by putting different parts together. You need to *think and search* through the book.

Author and You

You can NOT find the answer in the story. You need to think about what the *author* tells you, what *you* already know, and how it connects.

On Your Own

You can NOT find the answer in the story.
You can answer the question *on your own* without reading the story.

INTEGRATE IT!

Now take the following *two* titles and try it for yourself.

Roller Coaster
Written and illustrated by Marla Frazee

Figure 11.2 *Roller Coaster* by Marla Frazee. Copyright © 2003. Reprinted by permission of Harcourt Publishing.

WHEEEEEEEEEEEEEEEE! Twelve people experience the thrills and excitement of a roller coaster. Most of the riders have been on a roller coaster before with the exception of one little girl. Will she enjoy the clickity, clackity of the tracks as it zooms and zips through the sky?

Roller Coaster

Written and Illustrated by Marla Frazee

Have you ever ridden a roller coaster?

What is the best part about riding a roller coaster?

When is it too late to change your mind about riding the roller coaster?

How many riders per seat on this roller coaster?

What steps must the riders go through before the roller coaster takes off?	If you were riding this roller coaster how would you feel when the ride was over?	Using your own words, how would you describe the ride on this roller coaster?	What sound words can you find to describe the ride on the roller coaster?

Hooway for Wodney Wat
Written by Helen Lester • Illustrated by Lynn Munsinger

Figure 11.3 *Hooway for Wodney Wat* by Helen Lester, illustrated by Lynn Munsinger. Jacket art copyright © 2002 by Lynn Munsinger. Reprinted by permission of Houghton Mifflin Company. All rights reserved.

Rodney Rat has trouble pronouncing his "r's" which makes him the easy target for teasing on the playground. When a new class bully arrives at school to torment all the children, Rodney Rat ends up saving the day in a surprising turn of events. His speech impediment comes in very handy.

Hooway for Wodney Wat

Written by Helen Lester

Was Camilla Capybara smarter than all of the other students? Why or why not?

Why did the students at P.S. 142 Elementary consider Wodney Wat their hero?

What did Wodney Wat have difficulty doing?

| How did Wodney act at school after all of the teasing? | What did Wodney ask the rodents to do during Simon Says? | What did Wodney imagine Camilla would do to him after she heard them speak? | How do you deal with bullies? | Can you think of a time when someone has teased you? What was the situation? |

LINK IT!

Try linking some of these newly published titles to this reading strategy.

Aunt Claire's Yellow Beehive Hair
Written by Deborah Blumenthal • Illustrated by Mary GrandPre

Annie only knows about her Aunt Claire through stories told by her relatives. "Aunt Claire had a throaty voice, sharp red painted nails, and was famous for the magical beauty creams cooked up in her kitchen." Annie decides to get to know her ancestors better by creating a special tribute book. With Grandma's help she collects dusty photos, faded letters, and touching stories for her book.

100th Day Worries
Written by Margery Cuyler • Illustrated by Arthur Howard

Jessica is a worrier. She really starts worrying when her teacher tells her that on the 100th day of school students need to bring in a collection of 100 things. Jessica stews the whole week trying to think of an idea for her collection. Luckily her family helps Jessica come up with the most creative collection of all.

A Fine, Fine School
Written by Sharon Creech • Illustrated by Harry Bliss

Mr. Keene, the school principal, decides that his school is so fine that students need to be attending all the time. He begins insisting that children come to school on weekends, holidays, and summertime. A student named Tille clues her well-intentioned principal into the fact that there is some value to children having free time. After all, without free-time dogs won't learn to sit; little brothers won't learn to swing; and Tille won't learn to climb up trees.

Cook-A-Doodle-Doo!
Written by Janet Stevens and Susan Stevens Crummel • Illustrated by Janet Stevens

Rooster has decided he is going to cook just like his great-granny the Little Red Hen. Luckily for him Pig, Iguana, and Turtle have volunteered to help. Rooster explains everything to the other animals as they mix the ingredients to finish the shortcake. Along the side border of the text, the author has included interesting facts about cooking. When the shortcake is finished they run into a problem, but it is nothing these animals can't fix.

The Name Jar
Written and illustrated by Yangsook Choi

Unhei recently moved to America from Korea and wants to change her name. She feels that her classmates will make fun of it because it is so unique. To help her come up with a suitable name her classmates start a name jar contributing a wealth of names she could choose for her own. This is a very sweet story of acceptance, team building, and self-worth.

A Story for Bear
Written by Dennis Haseley • Illustrated by Jim LaMarche

A bear wonders about the strange marks he finds on a piece of paper in the woods. He strikes up an unlikely friendship with a woman who seems to be able to decipher the markings as she reads in the forest. Each day the bear returns to watch her read, sneaking closer and closer to observe what she is doing. One day the woman coaxes him close enough to listen to the stories. Throughout the autumn he returns day after day enjoying the magic of books and reading. When winter arrives the woman leaves her books for the bear with an unspoken promise that she will return to read to him again.

The Raft
Written and illustrated by Jim LaMarche

Nicky is reluctant to spend the summer with his grandmother in the country, especially since there will be no television. Just when he thinks he is about to die of boredom, he finds a raft that has wonderful drawings on it. This raft leads him to love the river, appreciate his grandmother, and discover a new talent he possesses.

The Memory String
Written by Eve Bunting • Illustrated by Ted Rand

Laura's mother passed away three years ago. Laura is having a hard time adjusting to having a new stepmother, Jane. One of Laura's most favorite things is a memory string created from the buttons from all the people in her mother's family. While avoiding helping with chores, Laura shows the string to her cat, which accidentally breaks the string scattering the buttons. After a frantic search, all but one of the buttons is located. The consequences of this event cause Laura to rethink her reluctance to embrace a relationship with her stepmother.

The Teddy Bear
Written and illustrated by David McPhail

A little boy loses a teddy bear that he loves a great deal. It was mistakenly thrown away and subsequently found by a man living on the streets. While the little boy mourns for his lost bear, the stuffed animal begins to enjoy his new life with the homeless man because he feels loved and needed. When the little boy visits the park and notices his lost bear with the homeless man, he has an important decision to make as he finally figures out where the bear truly belongs.

Sorry
Written by Jean Van Leeuwen • Illustrated by Brad Sneed

Two brothers who live together on a farm have an argument. Neither brother is big enough to apologize so they stop speaking to each other. This fight leads to the men dividing up the farm and moving apart. They continue with their lives and never speak even after marrying and having children. The anger builds between the families until finally one day their great-grandsons finally learn the power of saying "I'm Sorry."

Freedom Summer
Written by Deborah Wiles • Illustrated by Jerome Lagarrigue

In 1964, Joe and John Henry are best friends who enjoy shooting marbles and swimming together. Because Joe is white and John Henry is black, the boys are very excited when the Civil Rights Act of 1964 is passed and they can finally swim together in the same swimming pool. Fortunately their friendship is strong because it takes more than a law to change the racism that lives in the hearts of many of the people who live in their town.

Prediction Word

Bibliographical Information	Grade level
Chataway, Carol. 2001. *Perfect Pet*. Toronto, ON: Kids Can Press.	K–2nd
Edwards, Pamela Duncan. 2001. *Clara Caterpillar*. New York: HarperCollins.	K–3rd
Edwards, Pamela Duncan. 2003. *Rosie's Roses*. New York: HarperCollins.	K–3rd
Frasier, Debra. 2000. *Miss Alaineus—A Vocabulary Disaster*. San Diego, CA: Harcourt, Inc.	2nd–3rd
Graham, Bob. 2000. *Max*. Cambridge, MA: Candlewick Press.	K–2nd
Hartman, Bob. 2002. *Wolf Who Cried Boy*. New York: Putnam's Sons.	1st–3rd
Keller, Laurie. 2003. *Arnie the Doughnut*. New York: Holt.	1st–3rd
Kurtz, Jane and Christopher. 2002. *Water Hole Waiting*. New York: Greenwillow Books.	K–2nd
Nolan, Lucy. 1999. *Lizard Man of Crabtree County*. New York: Marshall Cavandish.	1st–3rd
Palatini, Margie. 2001. *Web Files*. New York: Hyperion Books.	2nd–3rd
Teague, Mark. 2002. *Dear Mrs. LaRue: Letters from Obedience School*. New York: Scholastic Press.	1st–3rd
Weston, Carrie. 2002. *Lucky Socks*. New York: P. Fogelman.	K–1st
Wheeler, Lisa. 2003. *Old Cricket*. New York: Atheneum Books for Young Readers.	1st–3rd

Character Chart

Bibliographical Information	Grade level
Bloom, Becky. 2001. *Crackers*. New York: Orchard Books.	K–3rd
Buehner, Caralyn. 2002. *Snowmen at Night*. New York: P. Fogelman.	K–3rd
Bunting, Eve. 1999. *Can You Do This Old Badger?* San Diego, CA: Harcourt.	K–3rd
Child, Lauren. 2002. *That Pesky Rat*. Cambridge, MA: Candlewick Press.	K–3rd
Daniels, Terri. 1999. *Feet in the Gym*. Delray Beach, FL: Winslow Press.	K–3rd
Dorros, Arthur. 2003. *City Chicken*. New York: HarperCollins.	K–3rd
Masurel, Claire. 2002. *Big Bad Wolf*. New York: Scholastic.	K–2nd
Nickle, John. 1999. *Ant Bully*. New York: Scholastic Press.	1st–3rd
O'Neill, Alexis. 2002. *Recess Queen*. New York: Scholastic Press.	K–3rd
Osborne, Mary Pope. 2002. *New York's Bravest*. New York: Knopf.	1st–3rd
Shields, Carol Diggory. 2002. *The Bugliest Bug*. Cambridge, MA: Candlewick Press.	K–2nd
Wheeler, Lisa. 2002. *Porcupining: A Prickly Love Story*. Boston, MA: Little Brown.	K–3rd

KWL Chart

Bibliographical Information	Grade level
Barner, Bob. 2001. *Dinosaur Bones*. San Francisco, CA: Chronicle Books.	K–2nd
Barton, Bryon. 2001. *My Car*. New York: Greenwillow.	K–1st
Chrustowski, Rick. 2000. *Bright Beetle*. New York: Holt.	K–3rd
Cowley, Joy. 1999. *Red-Eyed Tree Frog*. New York: Scholastic.	K–1st
Ehlert, Lois. 2001. *Waiting for Wings*. San Diego, CA: Harcourt.	K–1st
Gibbons, Gail. 2000. *Apples*. New York: Holiday House.	K–3rd
Gibbons, Gail. 2000. *My Soccer Book*. New York: HarperCollins.	1st–3rd
Jenkins, Martin. 1999. *Emperor's Egg*. Cambridge, MA: Candlewick Press.	K–3rd
Krull, Kathleen. 2001. *Supermarket*. New York: Holiday House.	1st–3rd
Linz, Kathi. 2002. *Chickens May Not Cross the Road and Other Crazy (But True) Laws*. Boston, MA: Houghton Mifflin.	2nd–3rd
Rex, Michael. 1999. *My Fire Engine*. New York: Holt.	K–1st
Schertle, Alice. 2002. *All You Need for a Snowman*. San Diego, CA: Silverwhistle/Harcourt.	K–2nd
Wallace, Nancy Elizabeth. 2001. *Taste of Honey*. Delray Beach, FL: Winslow Press.	1st–3rd

Sequence

Bibliographical Information	Grade level
Brown, Ken. 2001. *Scarecrow's Hat*. Atlanta, GA: Peachtree.	K–3rd
Casanova, Mary. 2003. *One-Dog Canoe*. New York: Farrar, Straus, and Giroux.	K–3rd
Crum, Shutta. 2003. *House in the Meadow*. Morton Grove, Ill: A. Whitman.	K–2nd
Crummel, Susan Stevens. 2003. *All in One Hour*. New York: Marshall Cavendish.	K–3rd
Feiffer, Jules. 1999. *Bark, George*. New York: HarperCollins.	K–2nd
Fox, Mem. 2002. *The Magic Hat*. San Diego, CA: Harcourt.	K–2nd
Gorbachev, Valeri. 2002. *One Rainy Day*. New York: Philomel Books.	K–2nd
Hort, Lenny. 2000. *Seals on the Bus*. New York: Holt.	K–3rd
Johnson, D.B. 2002. *Henry Builds a Cabin*. Boston, MA: Houghton Mifflin.	K–3rd
Taback, Simms. 1999. *Joseph Had a Little Overcoat*. New York: Viking.	K–2nd
Taback, Simms. 2002. *This is the House That Jack Built*. New York: Putnam's Sons.	K–2nd
Wilson, Karma. 2002. *Bear Snores On*. New York: Margaret K. McElderry Books.	K–3rd
Yolen, Jane. 2000. *Off We Go*. Boston, MA: Little, Brown, and Company.	K–1st

Circular Sequence Story Chart

Bibliographical Information	Grade level
Axtell, David. 2000. *We're Going on a Lion Hunt*. New York: Holt.	K–2nd
Dragonwagon, Crescent. 2003. *And Then It Rained . . . .* New York: Atheneum Books for Young Readers.	1st–3rd
Hubbell, Will. 2000. *Pumpkin Jack*. Morton Grove, Ill: A. Whitman.	K–3rd
Numeroff, Laura. 2000. *If You Take a Mouse to the Movies*. New York: Laura Geringer Books.	K–3rd
Numeroff, Laura. 2002. *If You Take a Mouse to School*. New York: Laura Geringer Books.	K–3rd
Schaefer, Lola. 2000. *This is the Sunflower*. New York: Greenwillow.	K–2nd
Schaefer, Lola. 2001. *This is the Rain*. New York: Greenwillow.	1st–3rd

Goal Structure Map

Bibliographical Information	Grade level
Brett, Jan. 2000. *Hedgie's Surprise*. New York: G.P. Putnam.	1st–3rd
Brown, Margaret Wise. 2001. *Dirty Little Boy*. Delray Beach, FL: Winslow Press.	K–2nd
Duffield, Katy. 2003. *Farmer McPeepers and His Missing Milk Cows*. Flagstaff, AZ: Rising Moon.	K–3rd
Ernst, Lisa Campbell. 1998. *Stella Louella's Runaway Book*. New York: Simon & Schuster.	1st–3rd
Emmett, Jonathan. 2001. *Bringing Down the Moon*. Cambridge, MA: Candlewick Press.	K–2nd
Fleming, Candace. 2002. *Muncha Muncha Muncha*. New York: Atheneum Books for Young Readers.	K–2nd
Hindley, Judy. 2002. *Do Like a Duck Does*. Cambridge, MA: Candlewick Press.	K–1st
Palatini, Margie. 2000. *Bedhead*. New York: Simon & Schuster.	1st–3rd
Palatini, Margie. 2001. *Tub-Boo-Boo*. New York: Simon & Schuster.	1st–3rd
Root, Phyllis. 2001. *Rattletrap Car*. Cambridge, MA: Candlewick Press.	K–2nd
Sturges, Philemon. 1999. *Little Red Hen Makes a Pizza*. New York: Dutton Children's Books.	1st–3rd
Tafuri, Nancy. 2001. *Silly Little Goose*. New York: Scholastic Press.	K–1st

Story Element Map

Bibliographical Information	Grade level
Banks, Kate. 2002. *Close Your Eyes*. New York: Frances Foster Books.	K–1st
Bateman, Teresa. 2001. *Farm Flu*. Morton Grove, IL: A. Whitman.	K–3rd
Bruss, Deborah. 2001. *Book! Book! Book!* New York: A.A. Levine.	K–2nd
Campbell, Ann. 2002. *Queenie Farmer Had Fifteen Daughters*. San Diego: Silver Whistle/Harcourt.	1st–3rd
Cronin, Doreen. 2000. *Click, Clack, Moo: Cows That Type*. New York: Simon & Schuster.	K–3rd
Helakoski, Leslie. 2002. *Smushy Bus*. Brookfield, CT: Millbrook Press.	1st–3rd
Mallat, Kathy. 2002. *Just Ducky*. New York: Walker.	K–1st
Rohmann, Eric. 2002. *My Friend Rabbit*. Brookfield, CT: Roaring Brook Press.	K–2nd
Root, Phyllis. 2003. *The Name Quilt*. New York: Farrar, Straus, and Giroux.	1st–3rd
Shannon, David. 2000. *The Rain Came Down*. New York: Blue Sky Press.	K–1st
Slangerup, Erik Jon. 2000. *Dirt Boy*. Morton Grove, IL: A. Whitman.	1st–3rd
Sloat, Teri. 1999. *Farmer Brown Goes Round and Round*. New York: DK Publishing.	K–3rd
Steen, Sandra and Susan. 2001. *Car Wash*. New York: G.P. Putnam's Sons.	K–2nd
Taylor, Alastair. 2001. *Swollobog*. Boston: Houghton Mifflin.	1st–3rd

T-Table

Bibliographical Information	Grade level
Bauer, Marion Dane. 2003. *Why Do Kittens Purr?* New York: Simon and Schuster.	K–1st
Bridges, Margaret Park. 2001. *Now What Can I Do?* New York: Sea Star Books.	K–1st
Brown, Margaret Wise. 2001. *Two Little Trains*. New York: HarperCollins.	K–1st
Collard, Sneed. 2002. *Leaving Home*. Boston: Houghton Mifflin.	K–1st
Corey, Shana. 2000. *You Forgot Your Skirt, Amelia Bloomer: A Very Improper Story*. New York: Scholastic Press.	2nd–3rd
Markes, Julie. 2001. *Good Thing You're Not an Octopus*. New York: HarperCollins.	K–1st
McCarty, Peter. 2002. *Hondo & Fabian*. New York: Holt.	K–2nd
Monks, Lydia. 1999. *The Cat Barked?* New York: Dial Books for Young Readers.	K–1st
Osborne, Mary Pope. 2000. *Kate and the Beanstalk*. New York: Antheneum Books for Young Readers.	1st–3rd
Rex, Michael. 2001. *The Pie is Cherry*. New York: Henry Holt.	K–1st
Rylant, Cynthia. 2000. *In November*. New York: Harcourt, Inc.	K–1st
Schlein, Miriam. 2002. *Hello, Hello!* New York: Simon & Schuster.	K–2nd
Stojic, Manya. 2002. *Snow*. New York: Knopf.	K–1st

Venn Diagram

Bibliographical Information	Grade level
Auch, Mary Jane and Herm. 2002. *Princess and the Pizza*. New York: Holiday House. Vaes, Alain. 2001. *Princess and the Pea*. Boston: Little, Brown.	1st–3rd 1st–3rd
Bunting, Eve. 2001. *Too Many Monsters*. Mahwah, NJ: Troll. Mayer, Mercer. 1968. *There's a Nightmare in the Closet*. New York: Dial Press.	K–1st K–1st
Downey, Lynn. 2000. *The Flea's Sneeze*. New York: Holt. Wood, Audrey. 1984. *The Napping House*. San Diego: Harcourt Brace Jovanovich.	K–1st K–1st
Huntington, Amy. 2001. *One Monday*. New York: Orchard Books. Hutchins, Pat. 1974. *The Wind Blew*. New York: Scholastic.	K–1st K–1st
Lowell, Susan. 2000. *Cindy Ellen: A Wild Western Cinderella*. New York: HarperCollins. Mitchell, Marianne. 2002. *Joe Cinders*. New York: Holt.	1st–3rd 1st–3rd
Lowell, Susan. 2001. *Dusty Locks and the Three Bears*. New York: Holt. Ernst, Lisa Campbell. 2000. *Goldilocks Returns*. New York: Simon & Schuster.	1st–3rd 1st–3rd
Palatini, Margie. 2002. *Earthquack!* New York: Simon & Schuster. Wattenberg, Jane. 2000. *Henny-Penny*. New York: Scholastic Press.	1st–3rd 1st–3rd
Root, Phyllis. 2002. *Oliver Finds His Way*. Cambridge, MA: Candlewick Press. Simmons, Jane. 2002. *Quack, Daisy, Quack!* Boston: Little, Brown.	K–1st K–1st
Vail, Rachel. 2002. *Sometimes I'm Bombaloo*. New York: Scholastic Press. Bang, Molly. 1999. *When Sophie Gets Angry—Really, Really Angry . . .* New York: Blue Sky Press.	K–1st K–1st
Whatley, Bruce. 2001. *Wait No Paint!* New York: HarperCollins. Wiesner, David. 2001. *The Three Pigs*. New York: Clarion Books.	1st–3rd 1st–3rd

Q.A.R. (Question–Answer Relationship)

Biographical Information	Grade level
Blumenthal, Deborah. 2001. *Aunt Claire's Yellow Beehive Hair*. New York: Dial Books for Young Readers.	1st–3rd
Bunting, Eve. 2000. *The Memory String*. New York: Clarion Books.	1st–3rd
Choi, Yangsook. 2001. *The Name Jar*. New York: Alfred A. Knopf.	1st–3rd
Creech, Sharon. 2001. *A Fine, Fine School*. New York: Joanna Cotler Books.	K–3rd
Cuyler, Margery. 2000. *100th Day Worries*. New York: Simon and Schuster.	K–3rd
Frazee, Marla. 2003. *Roller Coaster*. New York: Harcourt.	K–3rd
Haseley, Dennis. 2002. *A Story for Bear*. San Diego, CA: Silver Whistle/Harcourt.	1st–3rd
LaMarche, Jim. 2000. *The Raft*. New York: HarperCollins.	1st–3rd
Lester, Helen. 1999. *Hooway for Wodney Wat*. Boston: Houghton Mifflin.	1st–3rd
McPhail, David. 2002. *The Teddy Bear*. New York: Holt.	1st–3rd
Stevens, Janet and Crummel, Susan Stevens. 1999. *Cook-A-Doodle Doo!* San Diego, CA: Harcourt Brace.	K–3rd
Van Leeuwen, Jean. 2001. *Sorry*. New York: Phyllis Fogelmen Books.	1st–3rd
Wiles, Deborah. 2001. *Freedom Summer*. New York: Atheneum Books for Young Readers.	2nd–3rd

References

Benson, V. and Cummins, C. 2000. *Power of retelling: Developmental steps for building comprehension.* WA: Wright Group/McGraw Hill.

DeFord, D. 2003. *Teaching for comprehension in reading grades K-2.* NY: Scholastic.

Keene, E.O. and Zimmerman, S. 1997. *Mosaic of thought.* Portsmouth, NH: Heinemann.

Ogle, D.M. 1989. The know, want to know, learn strategy. In K.D. Muth (Ed.), *Children's comprehension of text.* (pp. 205–223). Newark, DE: International Reading Association.

Owocki, G. 2003. *Comprehension: strategic instruction for K-3 students.* Portsmouth, NH: Heinemann.

Raphael, T.E. 1984. Teaching learners about sources of information for answering comprehension questions. *Journal of Reading,* 27(4), 303–311.

Walker, B. 1992. *Supporting struggling readers.* Ontario: Pippin Publishing.

Index

100th Day Worries, 132

Activating prior knowledge, 2, 25, 33–34
All in One Hour, 53
All You Need for a Snowman, 37
And Then it Rained . . ., 62
Ant Bully, The, 31
Apples, 35
Arnie the Doughnut, 23
Auch, Mary Jane, 111
Aunt Claire's Yellow Beehive Hair, 132
Axtell, David, 62

Bang, Molly, 115
Banks, Kate, 91
Bark, George, 53
Barner, Bob, 34
Barton, Byron, 37
Bateman, Teresa, 92
Bauer, Marion Dane, 106
Bear Snores On, 54
Bedhead, 75
Big Bad Wolf, 31
Bloom, Becky, 30
Blumenthal, Deborah, 132
Book! Book! Book!, 91
Brett, Jan, 76
Bridges, Margaret Park, 105
Bright Beetle, 38
Bringing Down the Moon, 72–74
Brown, Ken, 48
Brown, Margaret Wise, 75, 105
Bruss, Deborah, 91
Buehner, Caralyn, 30
Bugliest Bug, The, 29
Building interest: using Prediction Word Bank, 2, 11–23; using Character Chart, 2, 25–31; using KWL Chart, 3, 33–38
Bunting, Eve, 30, 114, 133

Campbell, Ann, 92
Can You do This Old Badger?, 30
Car, My, 37
Car Wash, 91
Casanova, Mary, 54
Cat Barked?, The, 105
Categorization of information: using T-Table, 5, 95–106; using Q.A.R., 6, 119–134
Character attributes, 2, 25
Character Chart, 2, 25–31
Character goals, 4, 63–64
Chataway, Carol, 19
Chickens May Not Cross the Road and Other Crazy (But True) Laws, 36
Child, Lauren, 30

Choi, Yangsook, 132
Chrustowski, Rick, 38
Cindy Ellen: A Wild Western Cinderella, 115
Circular Sequence Story Chart, 4, 55–62
City Chicken, 31
Clara Caterpillar, 22
Click, Clack, Moo: Cows That Type, 91
Close Your Eyes, 91
Collard, Sneed B., 96
Compare and contrast; using T-table 5, 95–106; using Venn Diagram, 6, 107–116
Comprehension questioning, 6, 119–134
Cook-A-Doodle-Doo!, 132
Corey, Shana, 106
Cowley, Joy, 37
Crackers, 30
Creech, Sharon, 132
Cronin, Doreen, 91
Crum, Shutta, 54
Crummel, Susan Stevens, 53, 132
Cuyler, Margery, 132

Daniels, Terri, 30
Dear Mrs. LaRue: Letters from Obedience School, 23
Dinosaur Bones, 34
Dirt Boy, 85–87
Dirty Little Boy, The, 75
Do Like a Duck Does, 75
Dorros, Arthur, 31
Downey, Lynn, 115
Dragonwagon, Crescent, 62
Duffield, Katy, 67
Dusty Locks and The Three Bears, 116

Earthquack!, 116
Edwards, Pamela Duncan, 22
Ehlert, Lois, 37
Emmett, Jonathan, 74
Emperor's Egg, The, 38
Ernst, Lisa Campbell, 76, 116
Expository text, 2, 33

Farm Flu, 92
Farmer Brown Goes Round and Round, 91
Farmer McPeepers and His Missing Milk Cows, 67–71
Feet in the Gym, The, 30
Feiffer, Jules, 53
Fine, Fine School, A, 132
Fire Engine, My, 37
Flea's Sneeze, The, 115
Fleming, Candace, 76
Fox, Mem, 54
Frasier, Debra, 19

Frazee, Marla, 126
Freedom Summer, 134
Friend Rabbit, My, 88–90

Gibbons, Gail, 35, 37
Goal Structure Map, 4, 63–76
Goldilocks Returns, 116
Good Thing You're Not an Octopus!, 105
Gorbachev, Valeri, 53
Graham, Bob, 22

Hartman, Bob, 22
Haseley, Dennis, 133
Hedgie's Surprise, 76
Helakoski, Leslie, 92
Hello, Hello!, 106
Henny-Penny, 116
Henry Builds a Cabin, 46–47
Hindley, Judy, 75
Hondo & Fabian, 106
Hooway for Wodney Wat, 129–131
Hort, Lenny, 54
House in the Meadow, The, 54
Hubbell, Will, 59
Huntington, Amy, 114
Hutchins, Pat, 114

If You Take a Mouse to School, 62
If You Take a Mouse to the Movies, 62
In November, 100–104

Jenkins, Martin, 38
Joe Cinders, 116
Johnson, D.B., 46
Joseph Had a Little Overcoat, 53
Just Ducky, 82–84

Kate and the Beanstalk, 106
Keller, Laurie, 23
Krull, Kathleen, 35
Kurtz, Jane and Christopher, 22
KWL Chart, 2, 33–38

LaMarche, Jim, 133
Leaving Home, 96–99
Lester, Helen, 129
Linz, Kathi, 36
Little Red Hen Makes a Pizza, The, 75
Lizard Man of Crabtree County, The, 16–18
Lowell, Susan, 115, 116
Lucky Socks, 19

Magic Hat, The, 54
Mallat, Kathy, 82
Markes, Julie, 105
Masurel, Claire, 31

Max, 22
Mayer, Mercer, 114
McCarty, Peter, 106
McPhail, David, 133
Memory String, The, 133
Miss Alaineus—A Vocabulary Disaster, 19–21
Mitchell, Marianne, 116
Monks, Lydia, 105
Muncha Muncha Muncha, 76

Name Jar, The, 132
Name Quilt, The, 92
Napping House, The, 115
New York's Bravest, 31
Nickle, John, 31
Nolan, Lucy, 16
Now What Can I Do?, 105
Numeroff, Laura, 62

O'Neill, Alexis, 30
Off We Go, 53
Old Cricket, 22
Oliver Finds His Way, 115
One Monday, 114
One Rainy Day, 53
One-Dog Canoe, 54
Osborne, Mary Pope, 31, 106

Palatini, Margie, 7, 23, 75, 116
Perfect Pet, The, 19
Pesky Rat, That 30
Pie is Cherry, The, 106
Porcupining: A Prickly Love Story, 29
Prediction skills, 2, 11, 25
Prediction Word Bank, 2, 11–23
Princess and the Pea, The, 111–113
Princess and the Pizza, The, 111–113
Pumpkin Jack, 59–61

Q.A.R.(Question–answer relationship), 6, 119–134
Quack, Daisy, Quack!, 115
Queenie Farmer Had Fifteen Daughters, 92

Raft, The, 133
Rain Came Down, The, 91
Rattletrap Car, 76

Recess Queen, The, 30
Red-Eyed Tree Frog, 37
Retelling: using sequence activities 3, 41–54; using circular story activities, 4, 55–62; using goal structure maps, 4, 63–76; using story element maps, 5, 77–92
Rex, Michael, 37, 106
Rohmann, Eric, 88
Roller Coaster, 126–128
Root, Phyllis, 76, 92, 115
Rosie's Roses, 22
Rylant, Cynthia, 104

Scarecrow's Hat, The, 48–52
Schaefer, Lola, 62
Schertle, Alice, 37
Schlein, Miriam, 106
Seals on the Bus, 54
Sequence, 3, 41–54; using circular stories, 4, 55–62
Setting a reason to read, 25, 33–34, 95
Shannon, David, 91
Shields, Carol Diggory, 29
Silly Little Goose, 75
Simmons, Jane, 115
Slangerup, Erik Jon, 85
Sloat, Teri, 91
Smushy Bus, The, 92
Snow, 105
Snowmen at Night, 30
Soccer Book, My, 37
Sometimes I'm Bombaloo, 114
Sorry, 133
Steen, Sandra and Susan, 91
Stella Louella's Runaway Book, 76
Stevens, Janet, 132
Stojic, Manya, 105
Story element map, 5, 77–92
Story elements, 2, 5–6, 11, 41–42, 77–78, 107
Story for Bear, A, 133
Story sense, 3–5, 41, 77
Sturges, Philemon, 75
Summarization, 5, 77
Supermarket, 35
Swollobog, 92

Taback, Simms, 53
Tafuri, Nancy, 75
Taste of Honey, A, 37
Taylor, Alastair, 92
Teague, Mark, 23
Teddy Bear, The, 133
There's A Nightmare in my Closet, 114
This is the House That Jack Built, 53
This is the Rain, 62
This is the Sunflower, 62
Three Pigs, The, 108–110
Too Many Monsters, 114
T-table, 5, 95–106
Tub-Boo-Boo, 76
Two Little Trains, 105

Vaes, Alain, 111
Vail, Rachel, 114
Van Leeuwen, Jean, 133
Venn diagram, 6, 107–116
Vocabulary, 2, 11

Wait No Paint!, 108–110
Waiting for Wings, 37
Wallace, Nancy Elizabeth, 37
Water Hole Waiting, 22
Wattenberg, Jane, 116
We're Going On a Lion Hunt, 62
Web Files, The, 23
Weston, Carrie, 19
Whatley, Bruce, 108
Wheeler, Lisa, 22, 29
When Sophie Gets Angry—Really, Really Angry . . . , 115
Why Do Kittens Purr?, 106
Wiesner, David, 108
Wiles, Deborah, 134
Wilson, Karma, 54
Wind Blew, The, 114
Wolf Who Cried Boy, The, 22
Wood, Audrey, 115

Yolen, Jane, 53
You Forgot Your Skirt, Amelia Bloomer, 106

About the Author

CHRISTINE WALKER is currently the Library Media Specialist at Arbor Creek Elementary in Olathe, Kansas. She has a Bachelors Degree in Elementary Education and a Masters Degree in Curriculum and Instruction. Before obtaining her Library Media Certification 5 years ago, Christine spent 9 years teaching primary children in Kindergarten, 1st and 3rd grade. Christine, husband Bill, and son Dylan, spend their spare time amusing themselves with the antics of their two cats Max and Cookie.